BUILDING THINKING SKILLS®
Book 3 – Figural

SERIES TITLES
BUILDING THINKING SKILLS®—PRIMARY
BUILDING THINKING SKILLS®—BOOK 1
BUILDING THINKING SKILLS®—BOOK 2
BUILDING THINKING SKILLS®—BOOK 3 FIGURAL
BUILDING THINKING SKILLS®—BOOK 3 VERBAL

SANDRA PARKS AND HOWARD BLACK

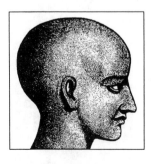

© 1985
CRITICAL THINKING BOOKS & SOFTWARE
www.criticalthinking.com
P.O. Box 448 • Pacific Grove • CA 93950-0448
Phone 800-458-4849 • FAX 408-393-3277
ISBN 0-89455-291-0
Printed in the United States of America

TABLE OF CONTENTS

A VERY IMPORTANT COMMENT ON THE IMPORTANCE OF CLASS DISCUSSION

The following activities were created with the hope that students would use *discussion,* not paper and pencil alone, to stimulate their perception and to develop their analysis skills. Although students may do activities individually in pencil-and-paper form, it is important to follow up each activity with class discussion to foster vocabulary development and to promote better transfer of thinking skills to content learning.

We encourage the use of manipulatives in introducing the exercises, for they provide students with a concrete basis for their discussions and a richer perception of the analysis tasks. For more detailed help, refer to the corresponding *Teacher's Manual and Lesson Plans* for this student book.

MATCHING FIGURES

Circle the figures that are the same in each row.

Example:

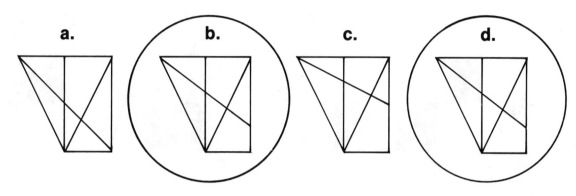

A-1

 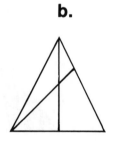 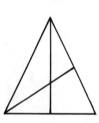 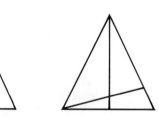

A-2

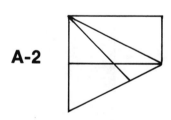 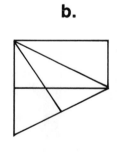 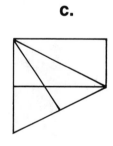 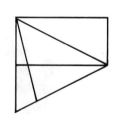

A-3

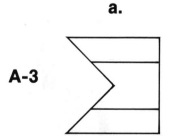 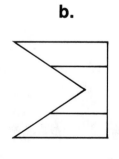 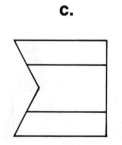 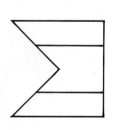

MATCHING FIGURES

Circle the figures that are the same in each row.

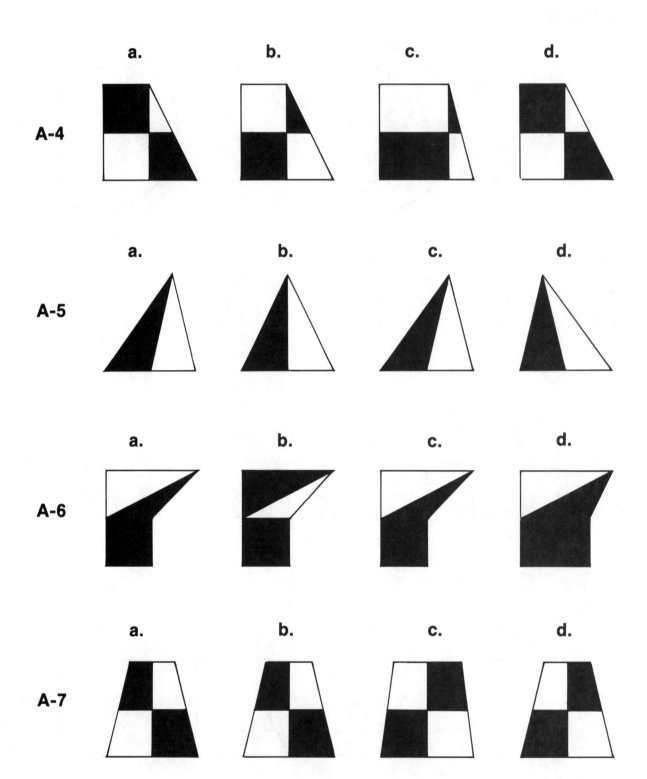

© 1985 MIDWEST PUBLICATIONS 93950

WHICH FIGURE DOES NOT MATCH?

Cross out the figure that does not match the other three figures in each row.

SIMILARITIES

EXAMPLE:

a. 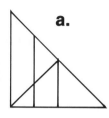 **b.** 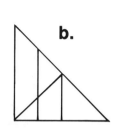 **c.** 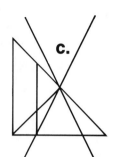 **d.**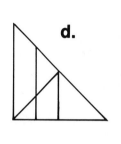

A-8

a.  **b.** 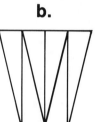 **c.** 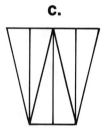 **d.**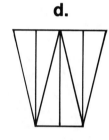

A-9

a. 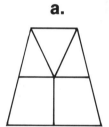 **b.** 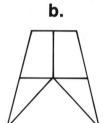 **c.** 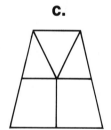 **d.**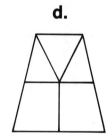

A-10

a. 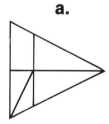 **b.** 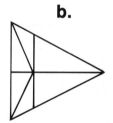 **c.** 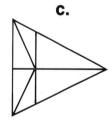 **d.**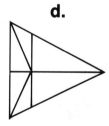

A-11

a. 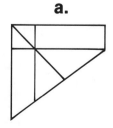 **b.** 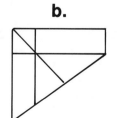 **c.** 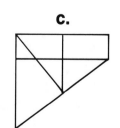 **d.**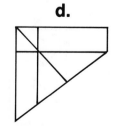

WHICH FIGURE DOES NOT MATCH

Cross out the figure that does not match the other four figures in each row.

	a.	b.	c.	d.	e.

A-12

A-13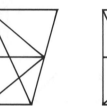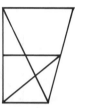

A-14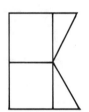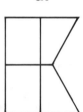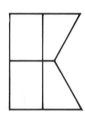

A-15

A-16

WHICH FIGURE DOES NOT MATCH

Cross out the figure that does not match the other four figures in each row.

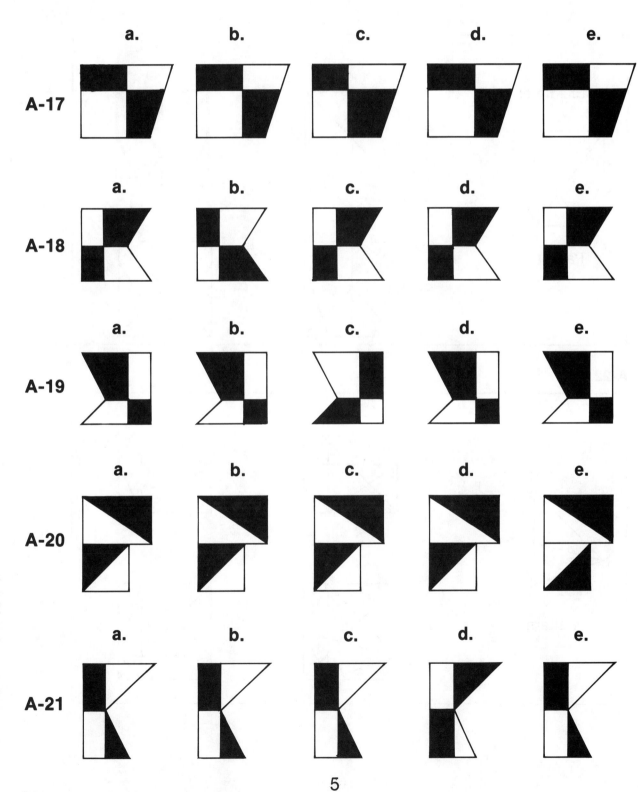

FINDING AND TRACING PATTERNS

Circle any figure that contains the pattern on the left. The pattern must be in the same position, but may have extra lines. Trace over the matching pattern to make sure you are right.

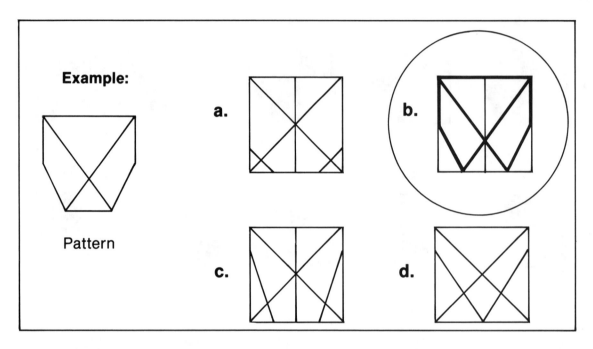

A-22

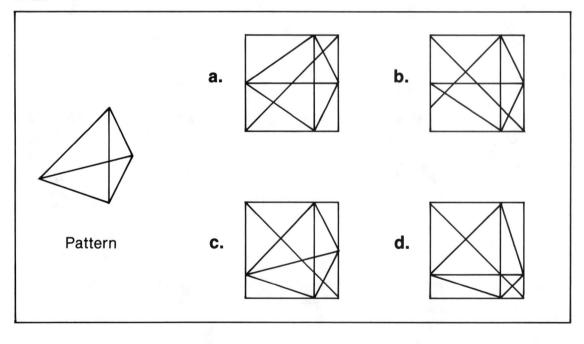

© 1985 MIDWEST PUBLICATIONS 93950

FINDING AND TRACING PATTERNS

Circle any figure that contains the pattern on the left. The pattern must be in the same position, but may have extra lines. Trace over the matching pattern to make sure you are right.

A-23

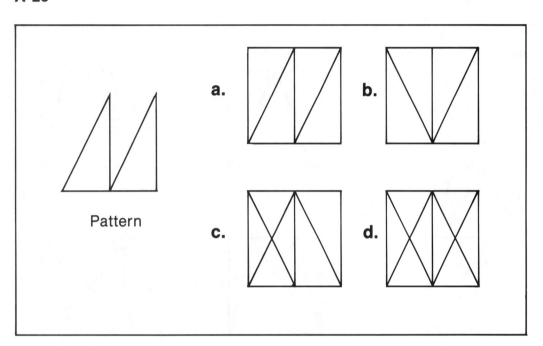

A-24

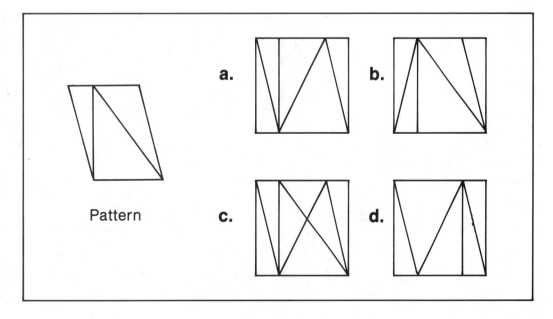

FINDING AND TRACING PATTERNS

Circle any figure that contains the pattern on the left. The pattern must be in the same position, but may have extra lines. Trace over the matching pattern to make sure you are right.

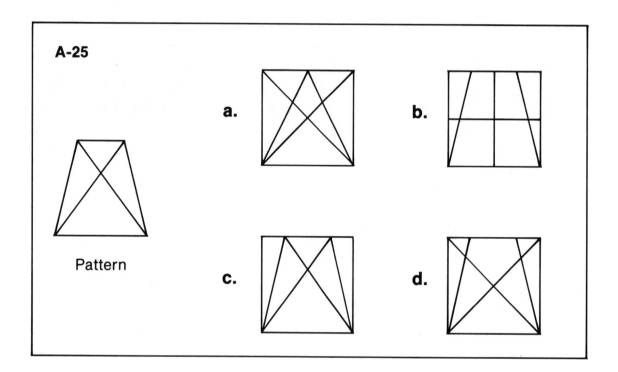

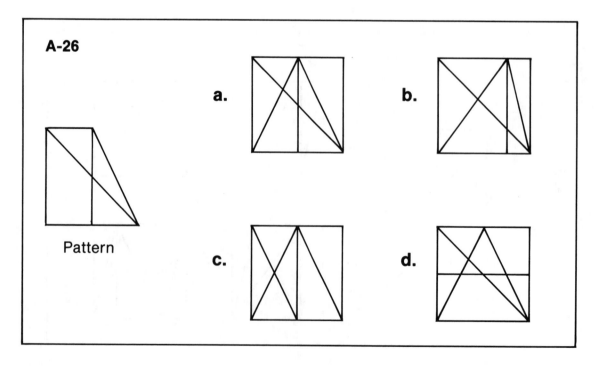

FINDING AND TRACING PATTERNS

Circle any figure that contains the pattern on the left. The pattern must be in the same position, but may have extra lines. Trace over the matching pattern to make sure you are right.

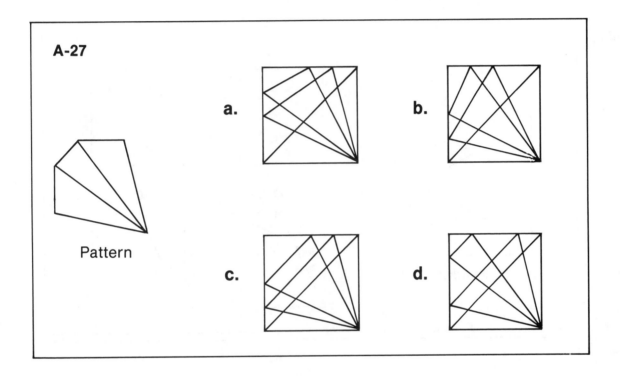

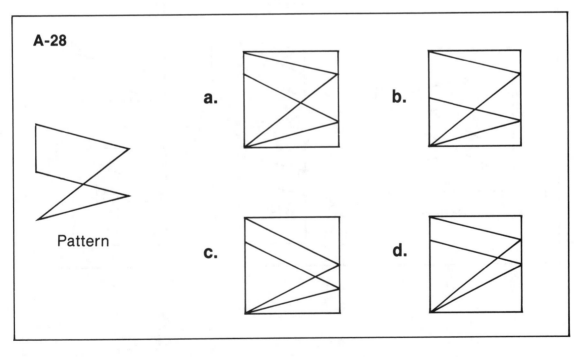

FINDING AND TRACING PATTERNS

Circle any figure that contains the pattern on the left. The pattern must be in the same position, but may have extra lines. Trace over the matching pattern to make sure you are right.

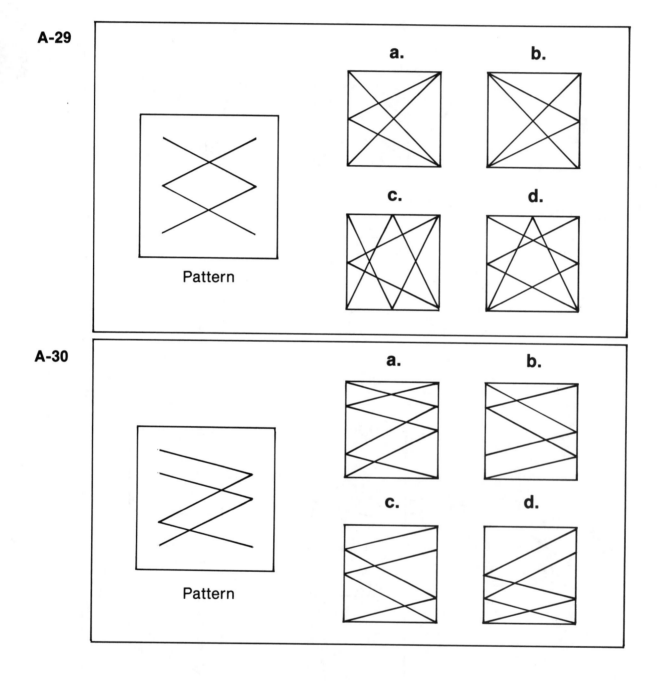

© 1985 MIDWEST PUBLICATIONS 93950

FINDING SHAPES

Check the shapes that you see in the figure on the left.

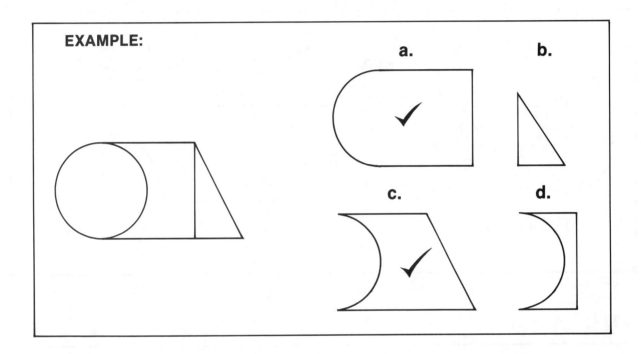

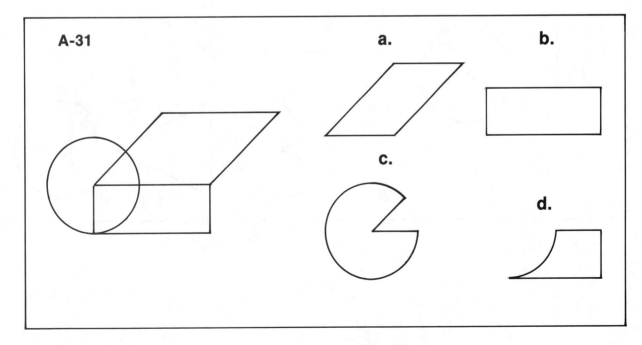

FINDING SHAPES

Check the shapes that you see in the figure on the left.

A-32

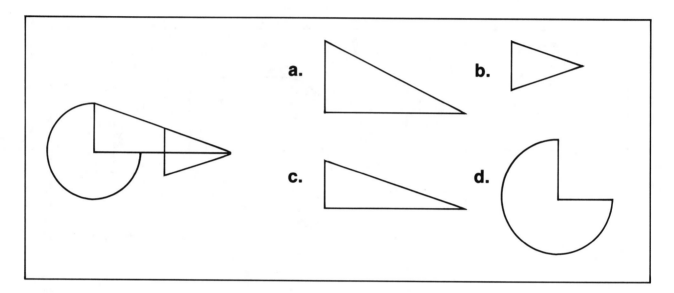

A-33

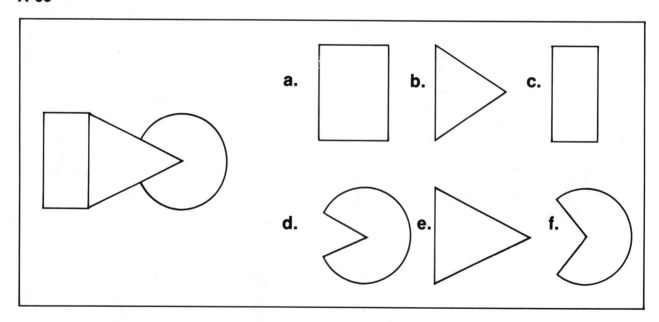

© 1985 MIDWEST PUBLICATIONS 93950

FINDING SHAPES

Check the shapes that you see in the figure on the left.

A-34

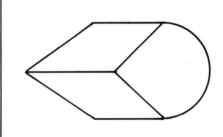

a.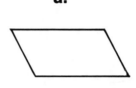

b.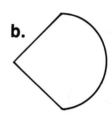

c.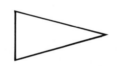

d.

A-35

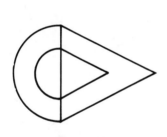

a.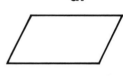

b.

c.

d.

A-36

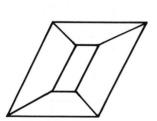

a.

b.

c.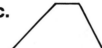

d.

COMBINING SHAPES

Check the figures that can be formed by joining the three
shapes on the left. The shapes may be moved in any direction.

EXAMPLE:

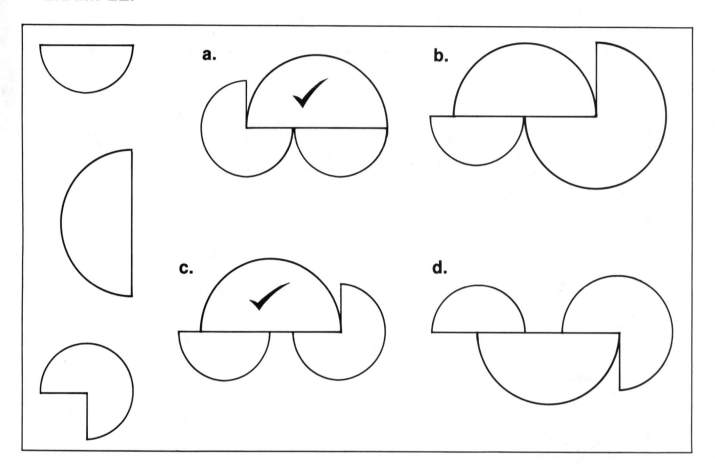

A-37

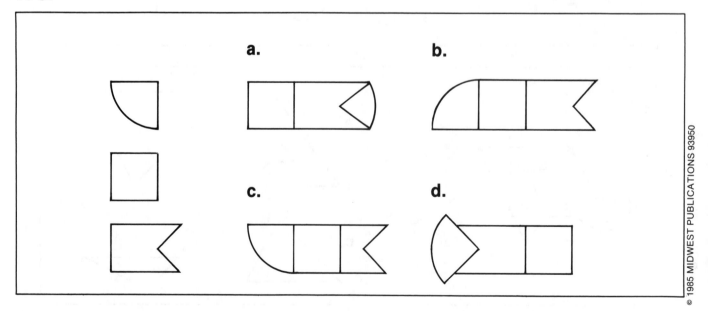

© 1985 MIDWEST PUBLICATIONS 93950

COMBINING SHAPES

Check the figures that can be formed by joining the three shapes on the left. The shapes may be moved in any direction.

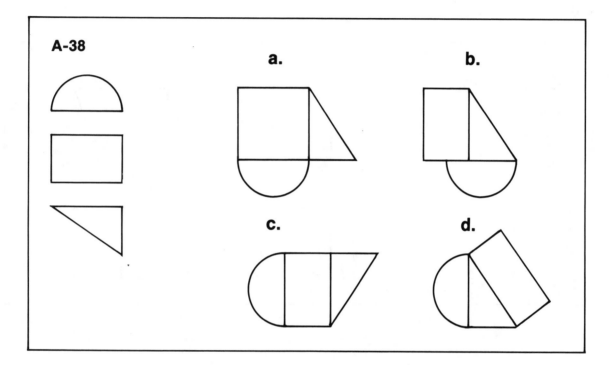

A-38

a.

b.

c.

d.

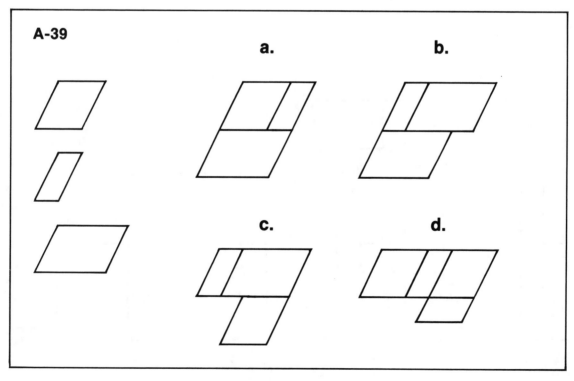

A-39

a.

b.

c.

d.

COMBINING SHAPES

Check the figures that can be formed by joining the three shapes on the left. The shapes may be turned in any direction.

A-40

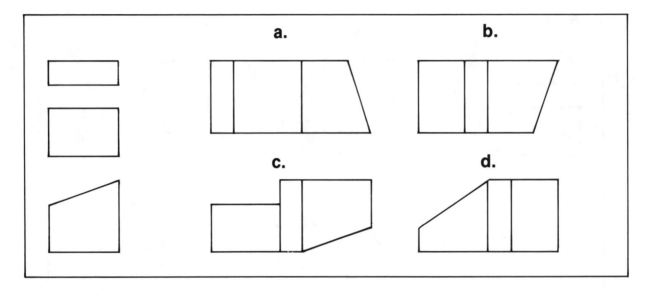

A-41

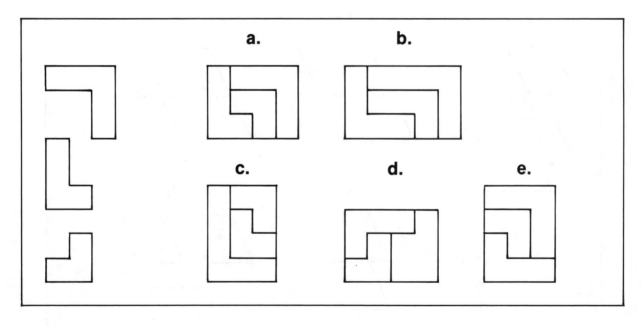

© 1985 MIDWEST PUBLICATIONS 93950

COMBINING SHAPES

Check the figures that can be formed by joining the shapes on the left. The shapes may be turned in any direction.

A-42

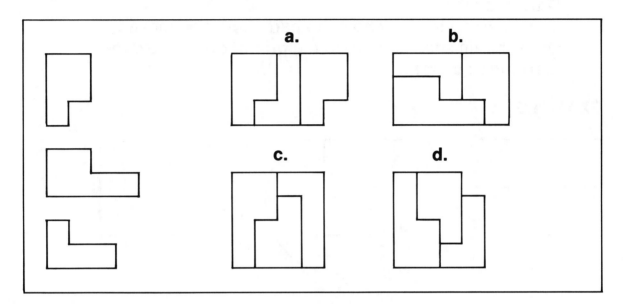

A-43

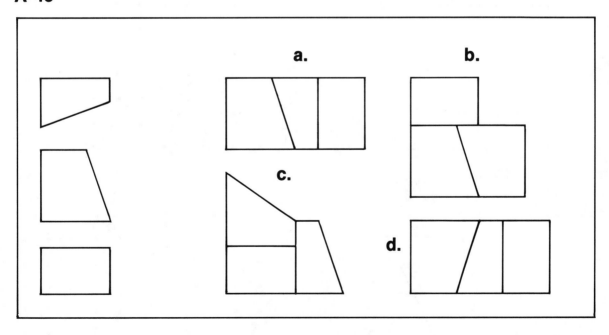

RECOMBINING SHAPES

Each of these figures can be cut once and rearranged to form a square.

1. Decide what part should be cut and moved.
2. Draw the cut line.
3. Use an arrow to show how the part should be moved.
4. Draw the finished square on the grid of dots (show the rearranged parts).

EXAMPLE:

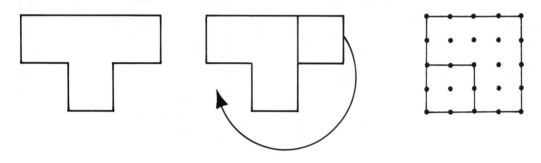

A-44

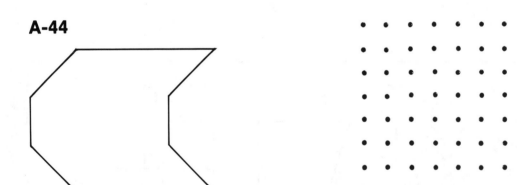

A-45

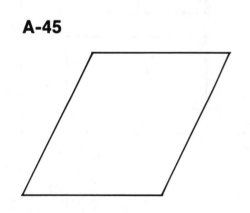
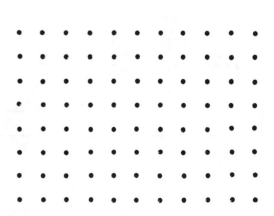

© 1985 MIDWEST PUBLICATIONS 93950

RECOMBINING SHAPES

Each of these figures can be cut once and rearranged to form a square. Draw the finished square on the grid of dots.

A-46

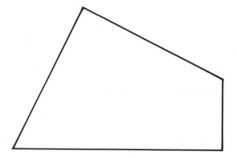

A-47

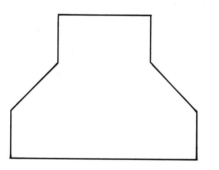

A-48

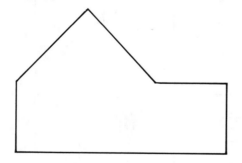

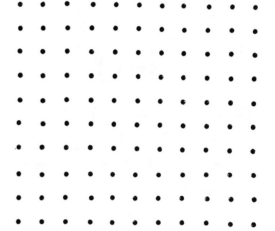

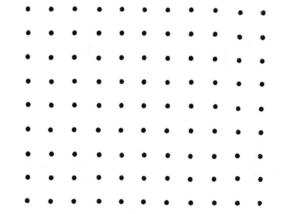

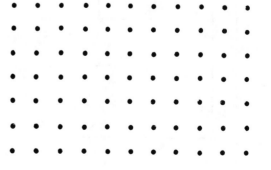

WHAT SHAPE COMPLETES THE SQUARE?

Circle the shape that completes the square. You may mentally move the shape in any direction.

EXAMPLE:

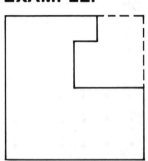

a.   b.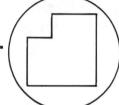

c.   d.

A-49

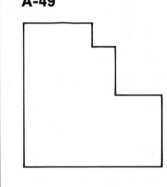

a.   b.

c.   d.

A-50

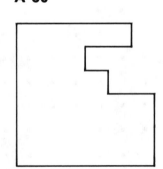

a.   b.

c.   d.

WHAT SHAPE COMPLETES THE SQUARE?

Circle the shape that completes the big square. You may mentally move the shape in any direction.

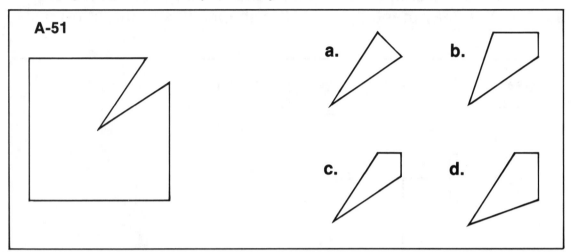

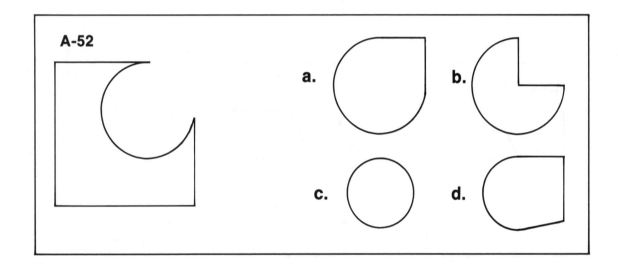

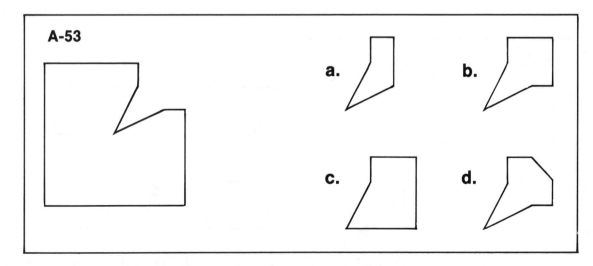

SIMILARITIES

COMPLETING THE SQUARE WITH TWO SHAPES

Circle the two shapes that will fill the missing area of the big square. You may mentally move the shapes in any direction.

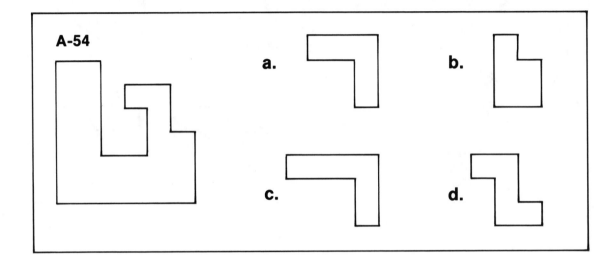

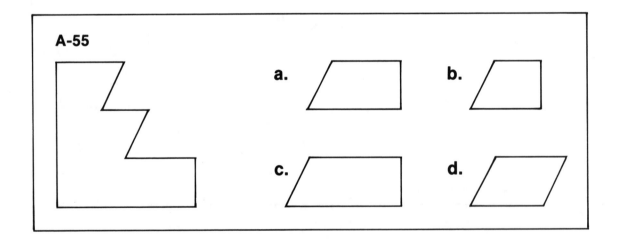

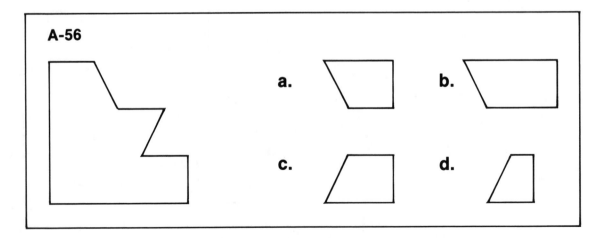

© 1985 MIDWEST PUBLICATIONS 93950

COMPLETING THE SQUARE WITH TWO SHAPES

Circle the two shapes that will fill in the missing area of the big square. You may mentally move the shapes in any direction.

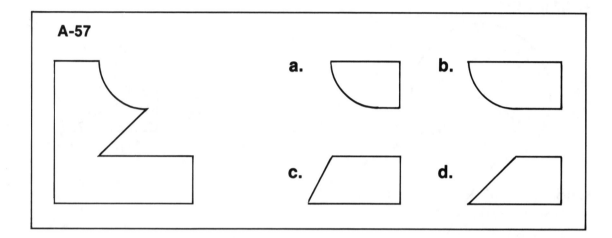

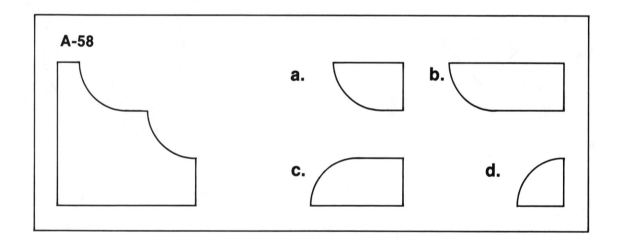

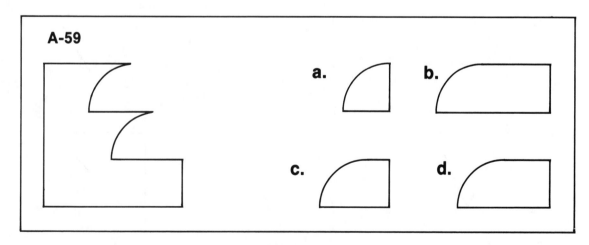

MATCHING CONGRUENT FIGURES

Congruent figures have the same shape and size. Position or direction does not affect congruence. Draw a line from each figure on the left to its congruent twin on the right.

EXAMPLE:

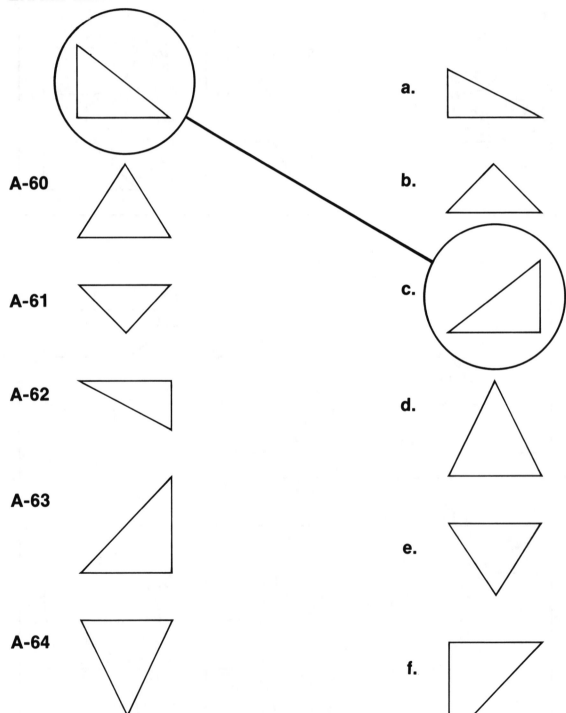

MATCHING CONGRUENT FIGURES

Congruent figures have the same shape and size. Position or direction does not affect congruence. Draw a line from the figure on the left to its congruent twin on the right.

A-65

a.

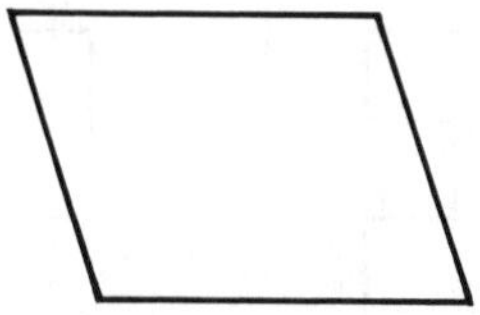

A-66

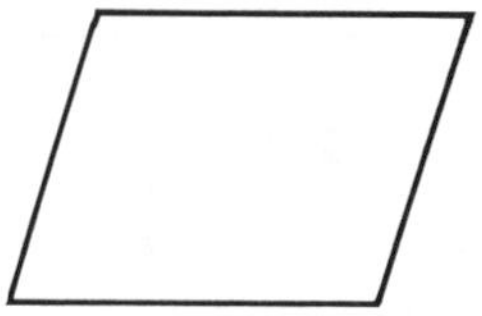

b.

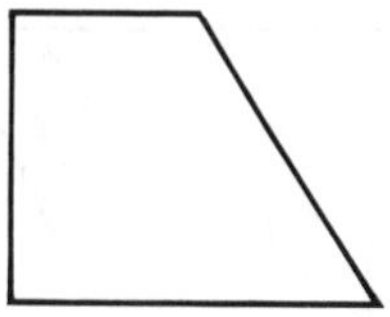

A-67

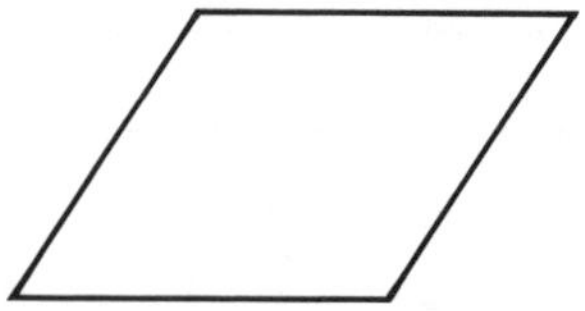

c.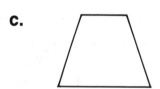

A-68

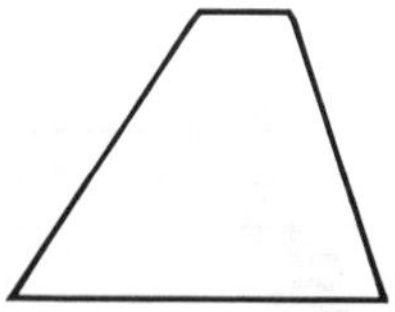

d.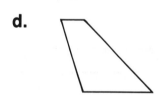

A-69

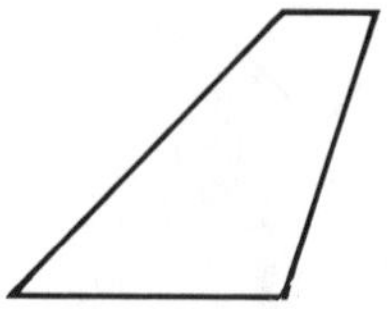

e.

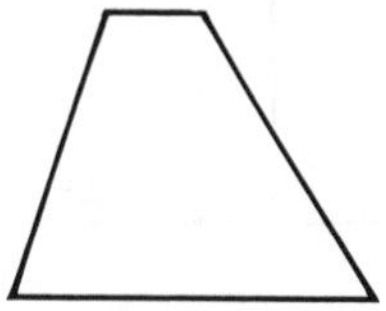

A-70

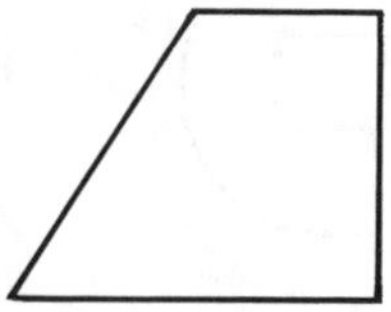

f.

WHICH FIGURE IS NOT CONGRUENT?

Cross out the figure that is not congruent to the first figure in the row.

EXAMPLE:

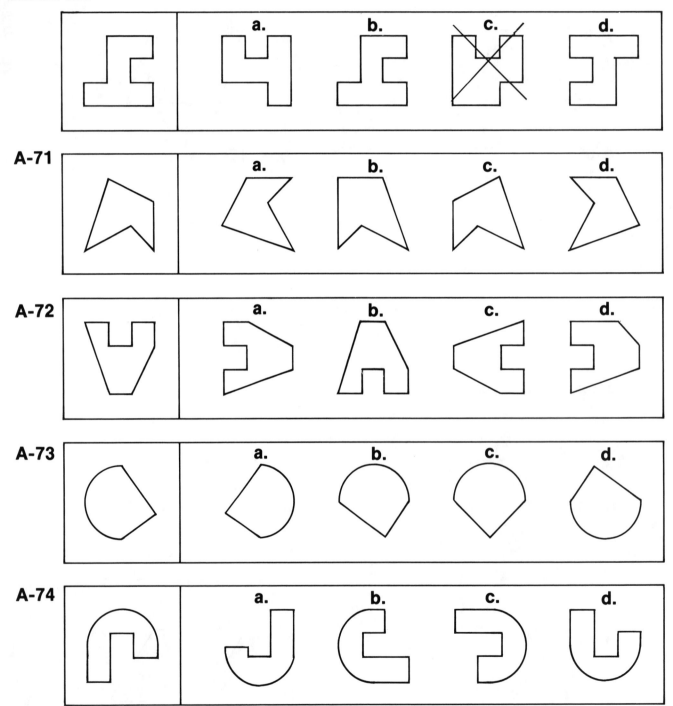

WHICH FIGURE IS NOT CONGRUENT?

Cross out the figure that is not congruent to the first figure in the row.

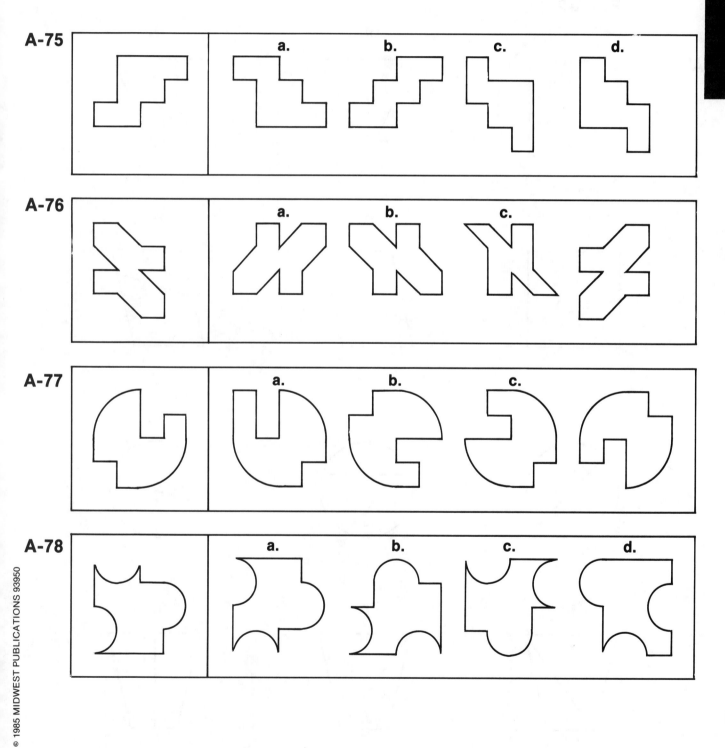

RECOGNIZING CONGRUENT PARTS

Circle the shapes that have been divided into congruent parts.
The parts may not face the same direction.

EXAMPLE:

A-79

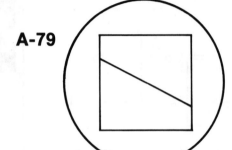

a.

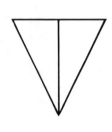

b.

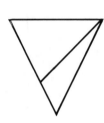

c.

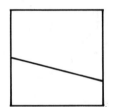

d.

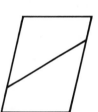

e.

f.

g.

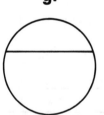

h.

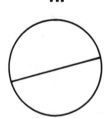

i.

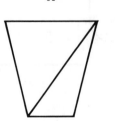

j.

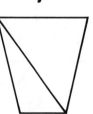

k.

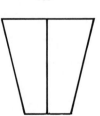

RECOGNIZING CONGRUENT PARTS

Circle the shapes that have been divided into congruent parts. The parts may not face the same direction.

EXAMPLE:

A-80

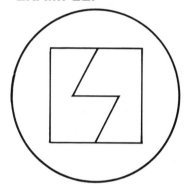

a.

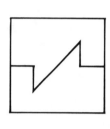

b.

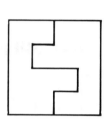

c.

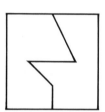

d.

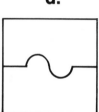

e.

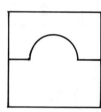

f.

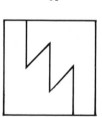

g.

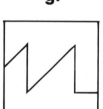

h.

i.

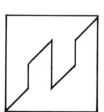

j.

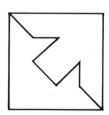

k.

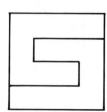

IDENTIFYING CONGRUENT PARTS

In the following designs, some parts are congruent; some are not. Use numbers or different colors to identify congruent parts.

EXAMPLE:

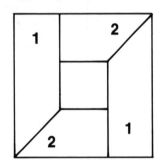

A-81

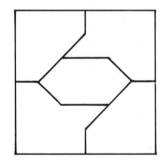

A-82

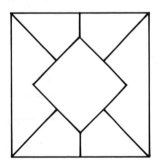

A-83

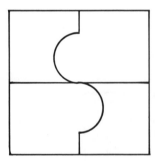

A-84

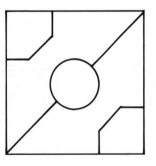

A-85

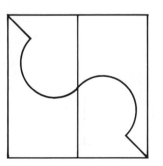

© 1985 MIDWEST PUBLICATIONS 93950

IDENTIFYING CONGRUENT PARTS

In the following designs, some parts are congruent; some are not. Use numbers or different colors to identify congruent parts.

A-86

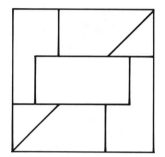

A-87

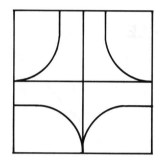

A-88

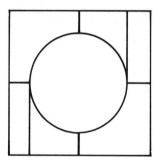

A-89

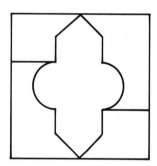

A-90

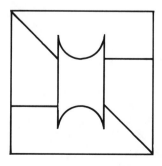

A-91

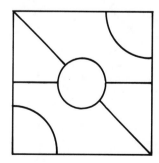

DIVIDING SHAPES INTO CONGRUENT PARTS

These triangles may be divided into congruent parts in more than four ways. The simplest division is to divide the figure into two congruent triangles (as in the example below). Divide the remaining triangles into **more than two** congruent parts. In each new pattern created by division into parts, all the parts must be congruent to one another. Do not repeat the same pattern.

EXAMPLE:

A-92

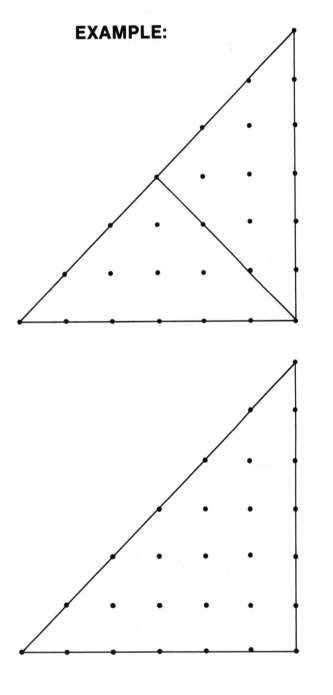

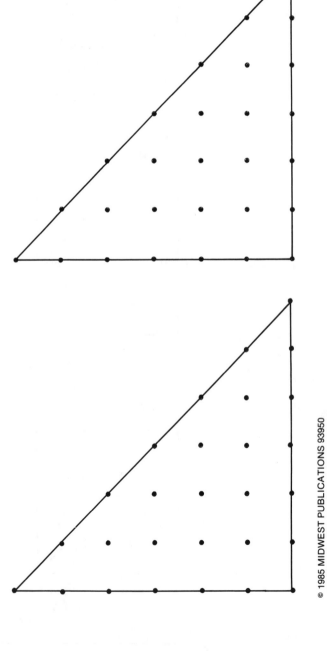

DIVIDING SHAPES INTO CONGRUENT PARTS

These octagons may be divided into congruent parts in more than four ways. Divide each octagon into **two or more** congruent parts. In each new pattern created by division into parts, all the parts must be congruent to one another. Do not repeat the same pattern.

A-93

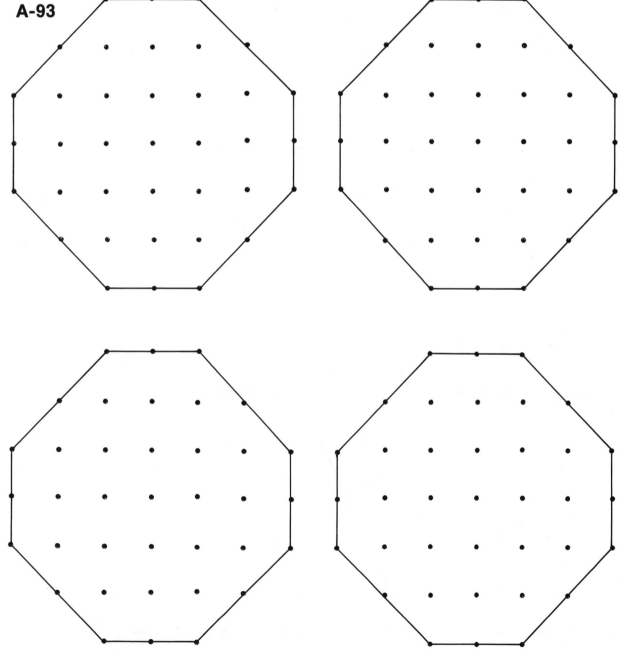

DIVIDING SHAPES INTO CONGRUENT PARTS

These parallelograms may be divided into congruent parts in more than six ways. Divide each parallelogram into **two or more** congruent parts. In each new pattern created by division into parts, all the parts must be congruent to one another. Do not repeat the same pattern.

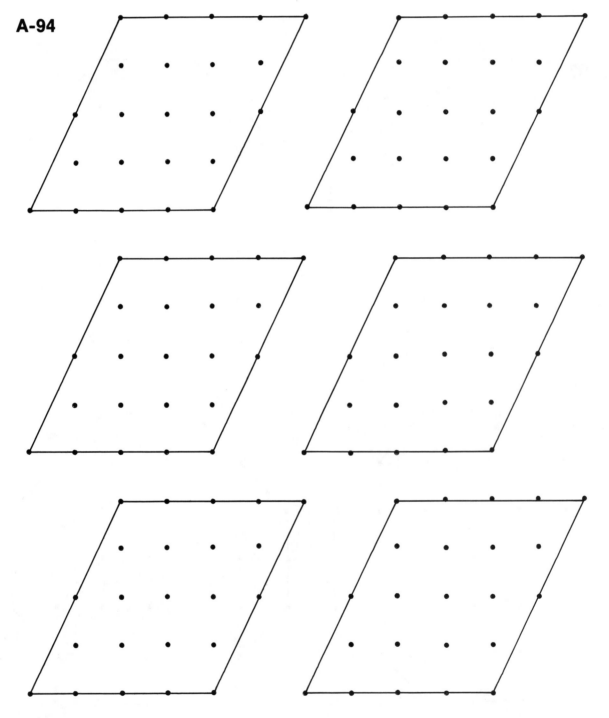

A-94

© 1985 MIDWEST PUBLICATIONS 93950

CONGRUENCE AND SIMILARITY

Two shapes are **congruent** if they have the same shape and the same size.

These two shapes are congruent.

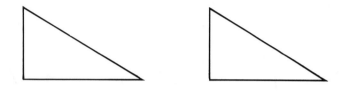

These two shapes are **not** congruent.

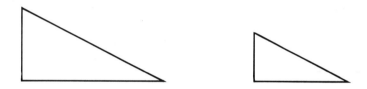

But, the shapes above are **similar** because, although they have different sizes, they have exactly the same shape.

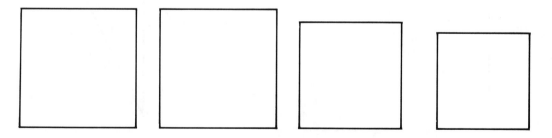

All the squares above are **similar** (because they have the same shape), but only the first two squares are **congruent** (because they have the same shape **and** the same size).

MATCHING SIMILAR FIGURES

Similar figures have the same shape, but different size. Draw a line from each figure on the left to a similar figure on the right.

EXAMPLE:

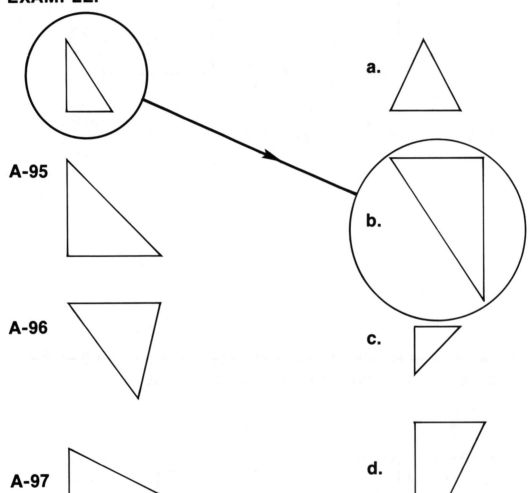

A-95

A-96

A-97

A-98

a.

b.

c.

d.

e.

MATCHING SIMILAR FIGURES

Similar figures have the same shape, but different size. Draw a line from each figure on the left to a similar figure on the right. Use the square grid to check proportions.

EXAMPLE:

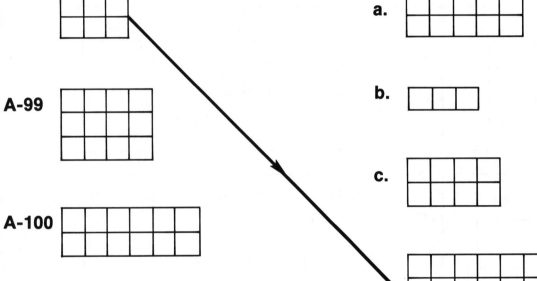

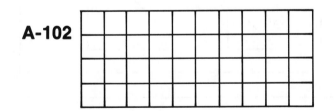

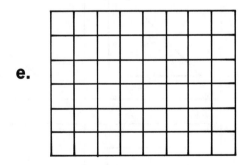

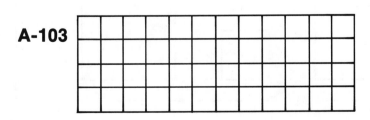

A-99

A-100

A-101

A-102

A-103

a.

b.

c.

d.

e.

f.

IDENTIFYING SIMILARITY AND CONGRUENCE

Mark each figure **S** if it is similar to the first one. Mark it **C** if it is congruent to the first one. Mark it **N** if it is neither.

EXAMPLE:

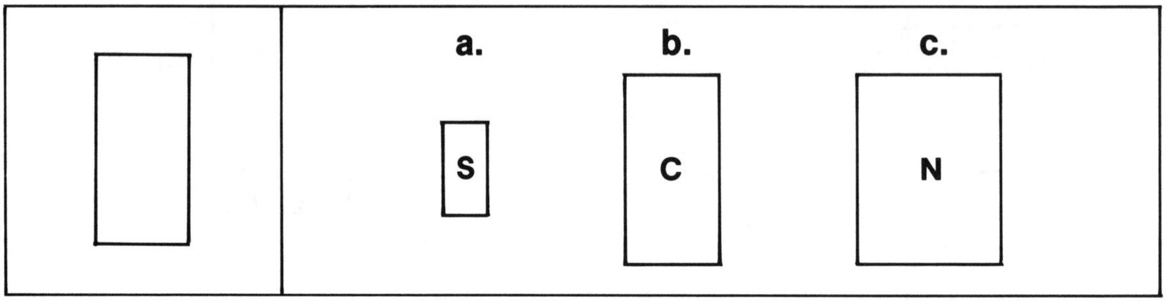

A-104

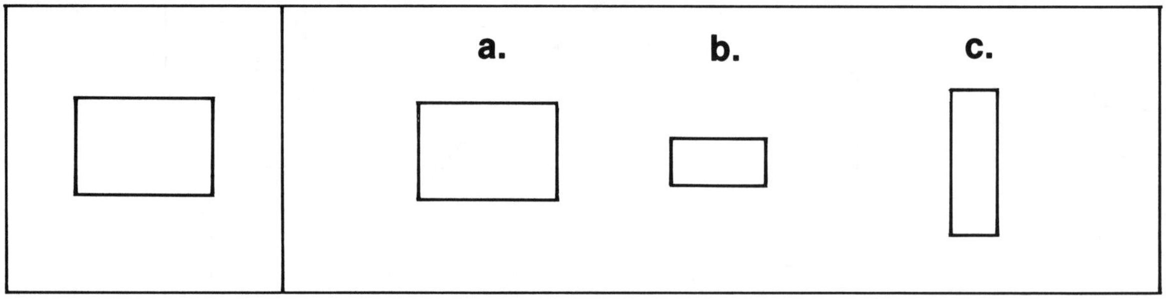

A-105

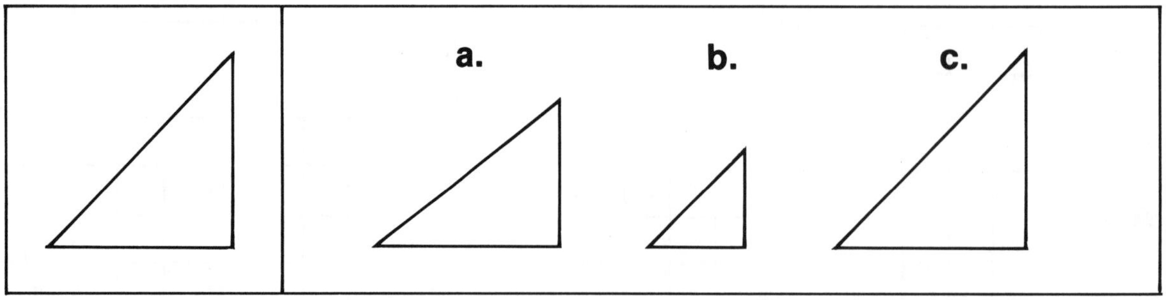

A-106

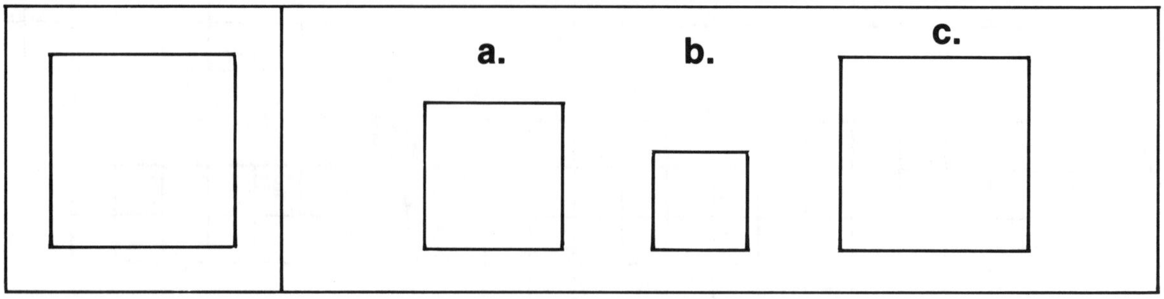

© 1985 MIDWEST PUBLICATIONS 93950

IDENTIFYING SIMILARITY AND CONGRUENCE

Mark each figure **S** if it is similar to the first one. Mark it **C** if it is congruent to the first one. Mark it **N** if it is neither.

A-107

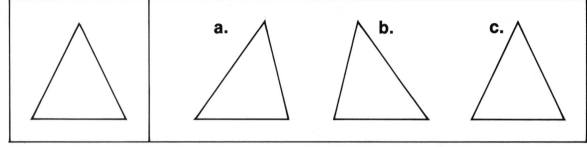

A-108

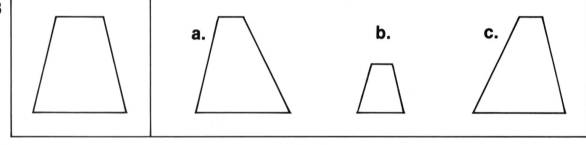

A-109

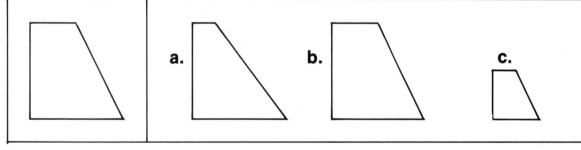

A-110

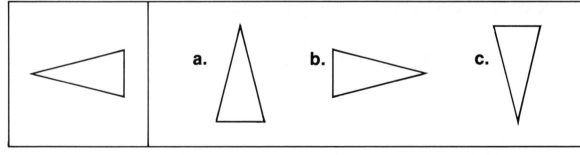

A-111

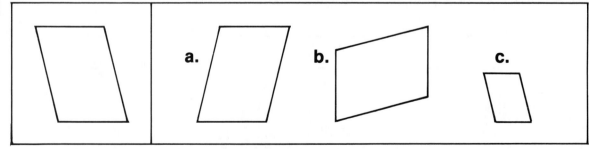

IDENTIFYING SIMILARITY AND CONGRUENCE

Examine the triangles below. Identify pairs of congruent triangles. Identify pairs of similar triangles.

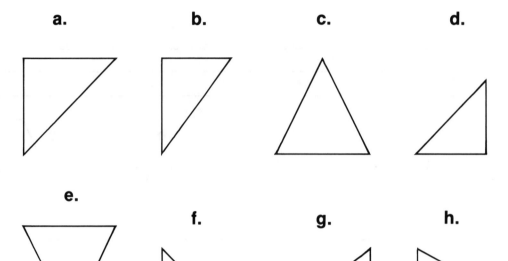

Which pairs of triangles are congruent?

EXAMPLE: Triangle "d" is congruent to triangle "f."

A-112   List other congruent pairs of triangles.

_____

A-113   Which pairs of triangles are similar?

_____

_____

© 1985 MIDWEST PUBLICATIONS 93950

IDENTIFYING SIMILARITY AND CONGRUENCE

Examine the parallelograms below. Identify groups of congruent shapes. Identify pairs of similar shapes.

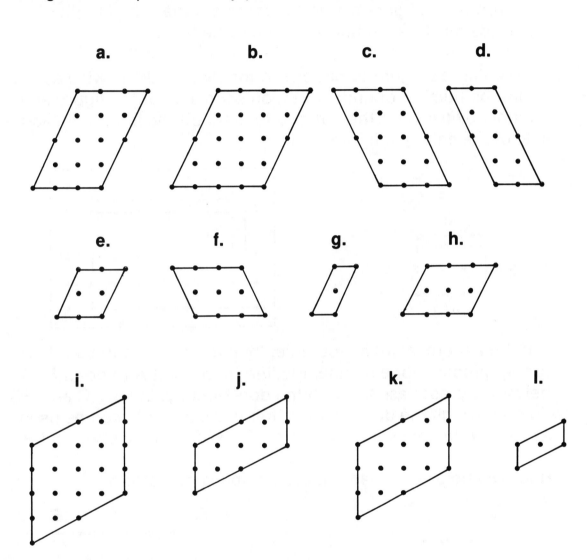

A-114 Which pairs or groups of parallelograms are congruent?

_____

A-115 Which groups of parallelograms are similar?

_____

_____

PRODUCING SIMILAR FIGURES — ENLARGING

To produce a figure that is similar to another, the length of each side must be multiplied by the same factor.

To enlarge a figure or pattern so that each side is twice as long, count the number of units (dots) on each side of the figure and multiply by two. Use the dot grid to mark off the length of each side of the enlarged figure.

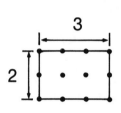

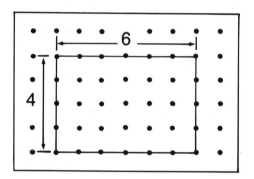

If the pattern is not a rectangle, then it is difficult to count units (dots) directly. For example, the line from point A to point B below does not pass through the dots directly. Lines AC and BC do go through the dots exactly; therefore, the dots can be used as a guide for measuring lengths AC and BC. If lines AC and BC are doubled, then the line AB will also be doubled. This "triangle rule" will help you enlarge more complicated patterns.

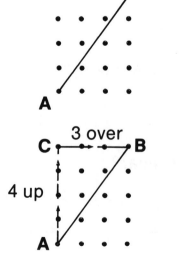

becomes

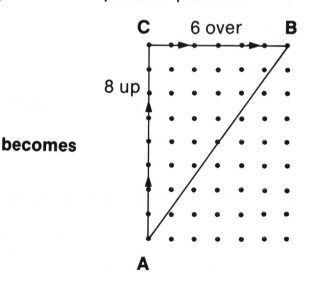

PRODUCING SIMILAR FIGURES—ENLARGING

Use the dot grid to draw a figure with sides twice as long as the figure on the left.

A-116

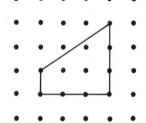

A-117

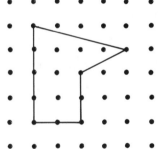

A-118

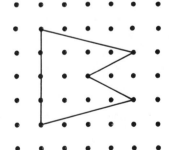

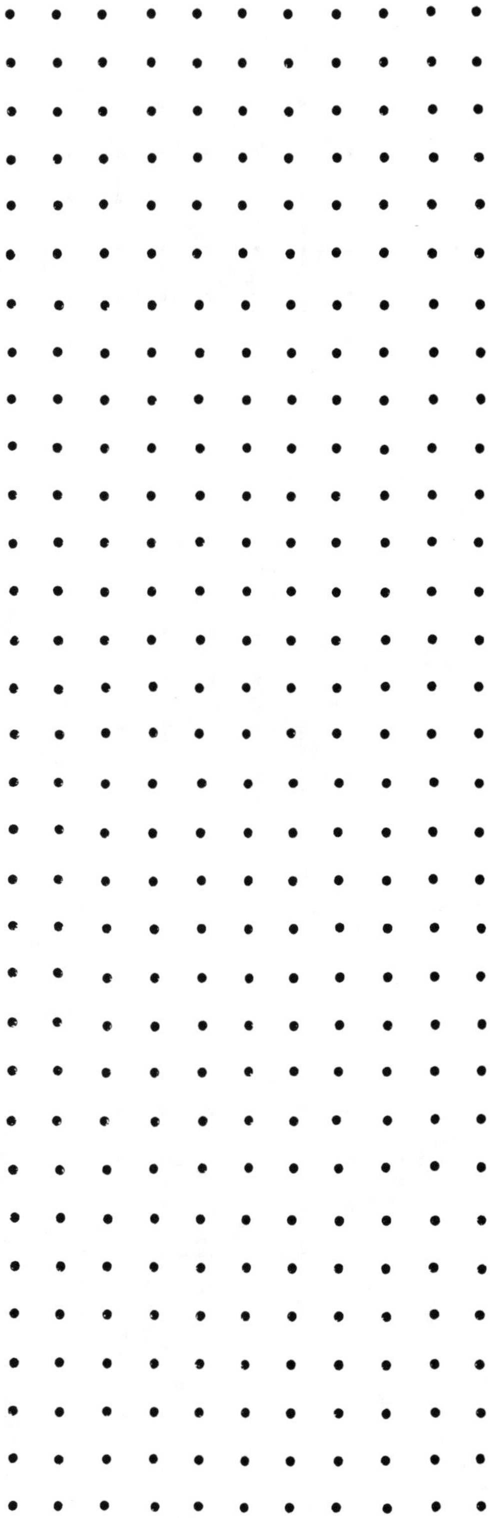

PRODUCING SIMILAR FIGURES—ENLARGING

Use the dot grid to draw a figure with sides twice as long as the figure on the left.

A-119

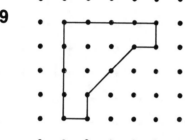 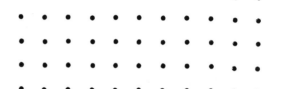

A-120

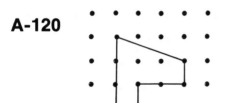 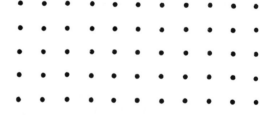

A-121

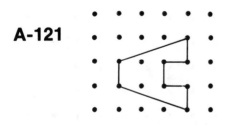 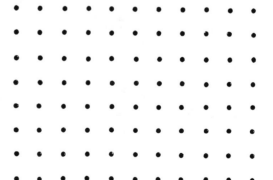

PRODUCING SIMILAR FIGURES—ENLARGING

To produce a figure that is similar to another, each side must be multiplied by the same factor.

To enlarge a figure so that each side is one and one-half (1½) times as long, count the number of units (dots) on each side of the figure and multiply by one and one-half (1½).

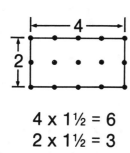

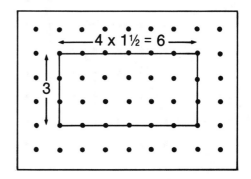

4 x 1½ = 6
2 x 1½ = 3

If the pattern is not a rectangle, then the "triangle rule" (see page 42) may be used.

EXAMPLE:

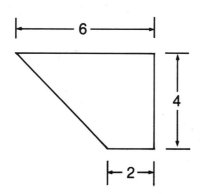

Second: Lay out the lengths on the grid

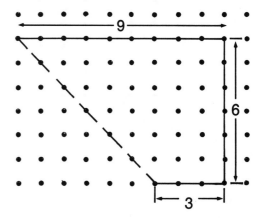

First: Multiply the lengths by 1½
2 x 1½ = 3
4 x 1½ = 6
6 x 1½ = 9

Third: Draw in the remaining side (shown by the dashed line)

(see page 42)

PRODUCING SIMILAR FIGURES—ENLARGING

Use the dot grid to draw a figure with sides one and one-half (1½) times as long as the figure on the left.

A-122

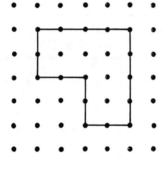

A-123

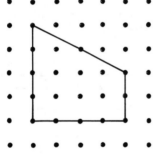

A-124

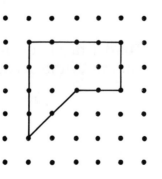

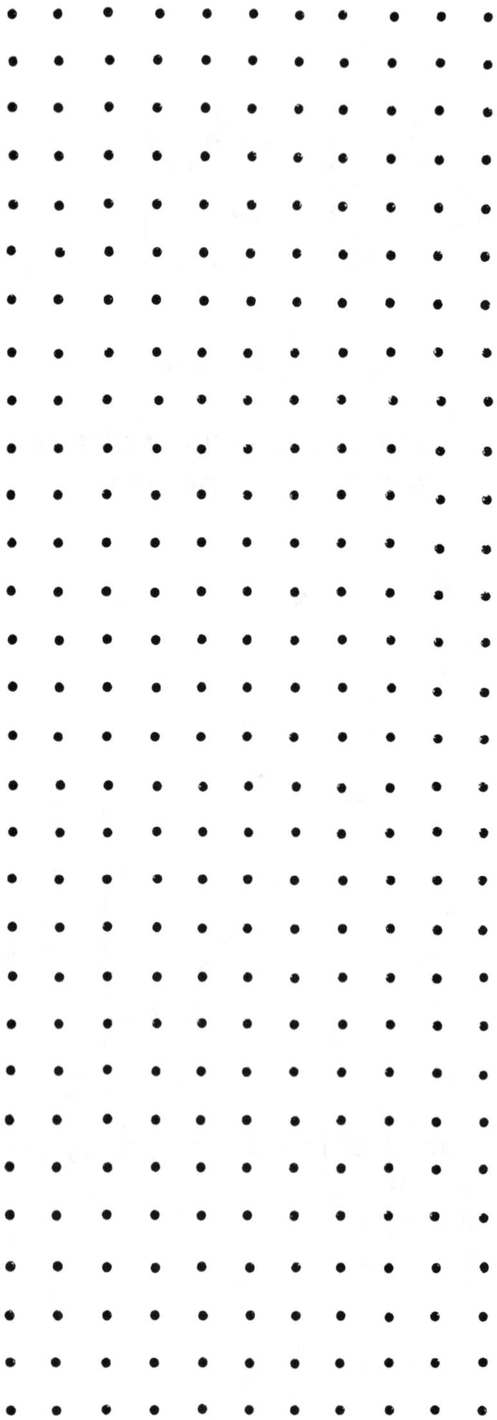

PRODUCING SIMILAR FIGURES—ENLARGING

Use the dot grid to draw a figure with sides one and one-half (1½) times as long as the figure on the left.

A-125

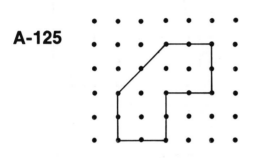
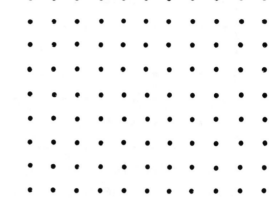

A-126

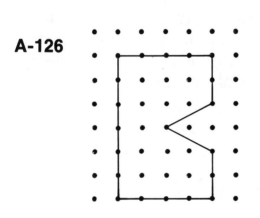
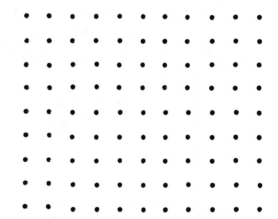

A-127

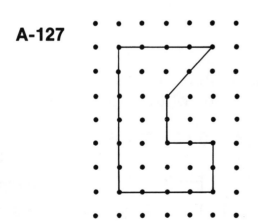

PRODUCING SIMILAR FIGURES—REDUCING

To reduce a figure or pattern so that each side is half as long, count the number of units (dots) on each side of the figure and divide by two. Use the dot grid to mark off the length of each side of the reduced figure.

Reducing a rectangle:

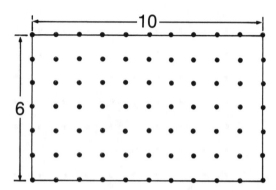
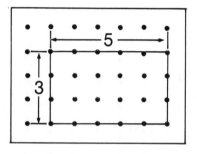

If the pattern is not a rectangle, then the "triangle rule" may be used to reduce the size of a line drawn at an angle.

Here is an example of the "triangle rule." Start at point A and go upward until your pencil is in line with point B. Then go over until your pencil is on point B. Next, count the dots and divide by two. Finally, draw the reduced figure as shown below.

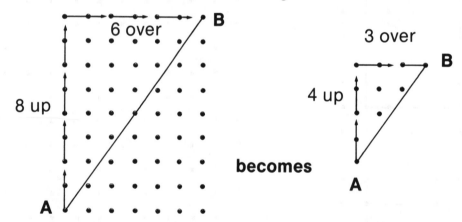

To reduce a figure so that each side is three-fourths (¾) as long, count the number of units on each side of the figure and multiply by ¾.

EXAMPLE: 4 x ¾ = 3 ; 8 x ¾ = 6

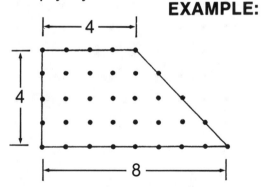
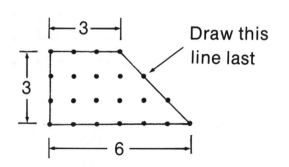

Draw this line last

© 1985 MIDWEST PUBLICATIONS 93950

PRODUCING SIMILAR FIGURES—REDUCING

Draw a figure with sides half as long as the figure on the left.
Use the dot grid as a measurement guide.

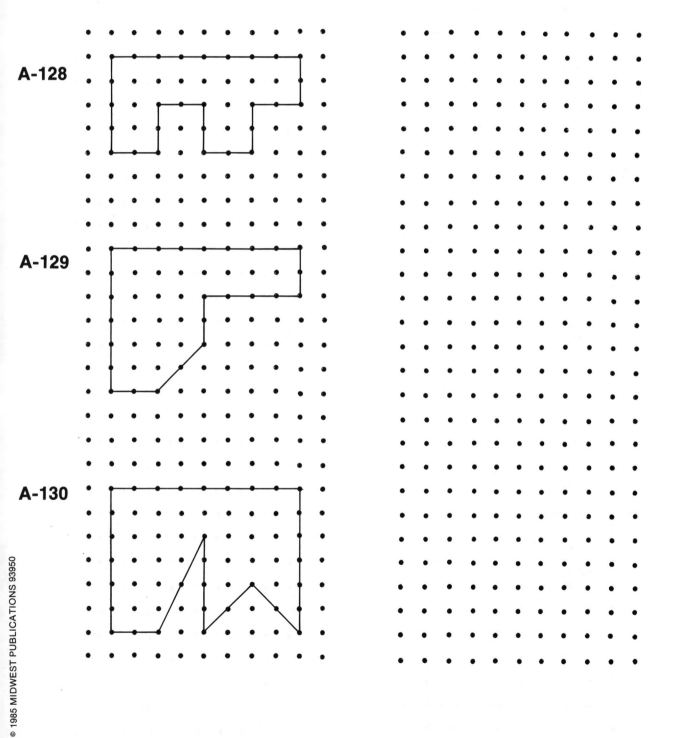

A-128

A-129

A-130

© 1985 MIDWEST PUBLICATIONS 93950

PRODUCING SIMILAR FIGURES—REDUCING

Draw a figure with sides half as long as the figure on the left.
Use the dot grid as a measurement guide.

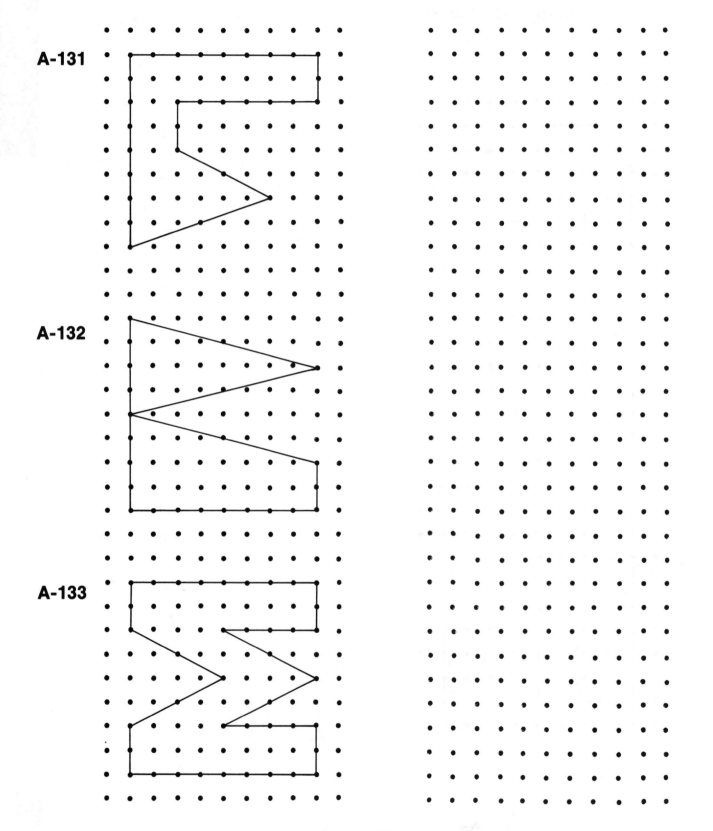

A-131

A-132

A-133

PRODUCING SIMILAR FIGURES—REDUCING

Draw a figure with sides three-fourths as long as the figure on the left. Use the dot grid as a measurement guide.

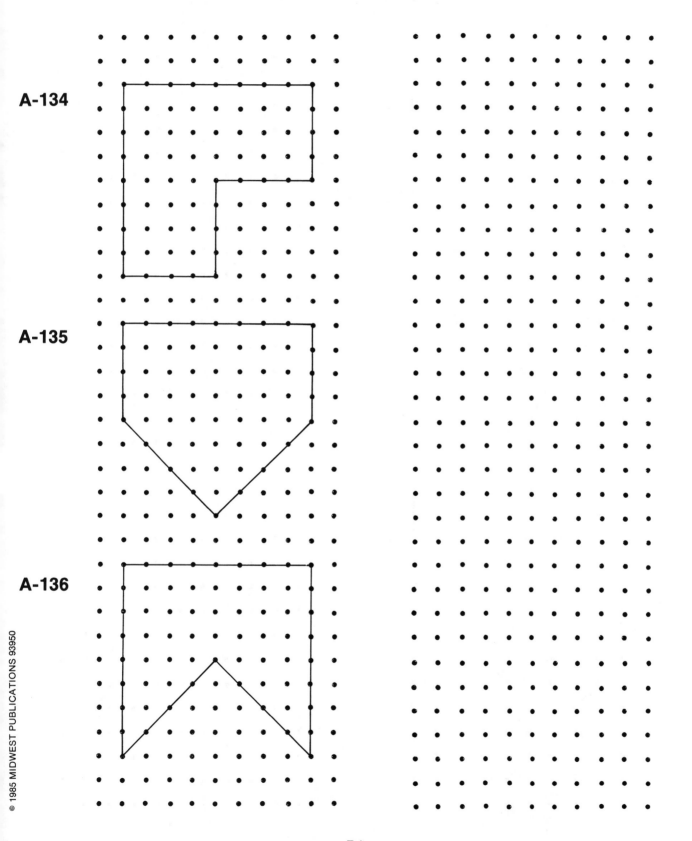

A-134

A-135

A-136

PRODUCING SIMILAR FIGURES—REDUCING

Draw a figure with sides three-fourths as long as the figure on the left. Use the dot grid as a measurement guide.

A-137

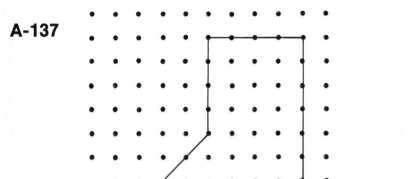
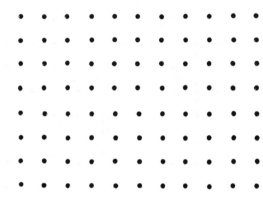

A-138

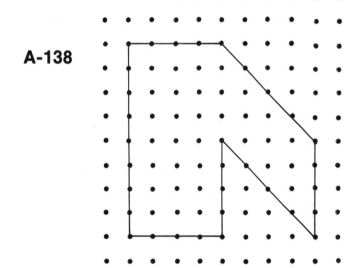
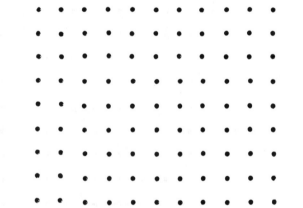

A-139

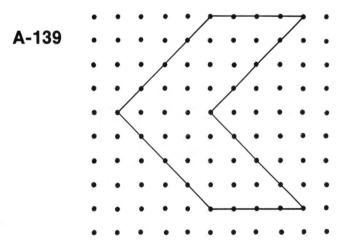

IDENTIFYING ENLARGEMENT AND REDUCTION

Compare figure B to figure A. Decide whether figure B has been enlarged or reduced and by what factor.

SIMILARITIES

EXAMPLE:

A. 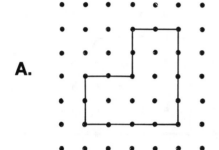   **B.**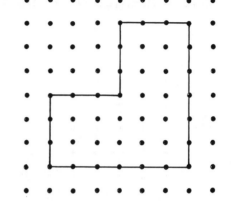

Each side of figure B has been ___enlarged___ to ___1½___ times as long.

A-140

A. 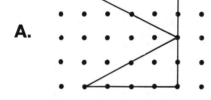   **B.**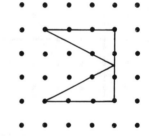

Each side of figure B has been _____ to _____ times as long.

A-141

A. 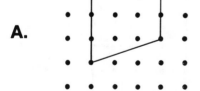   **B.**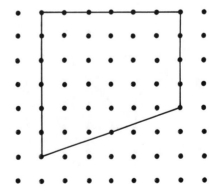

Each side of figure B has been _____ to _____ times as long.

IDENTIFYING ENLARGEMENT AND REDUCTION

Compare figure B to figure A. Decide whether figure B has been enlarged or reduced and by what factor.

A-142

A. 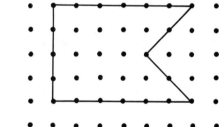　　　**B.**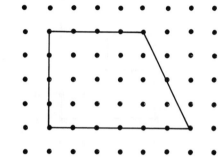

Each side of figure B has been _____ to

_____ times as long.

A-143

A. 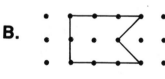　　　**B.**

Each side of figure B has been _____ to

_____ times as long.

A-144

A. 　　　**B.**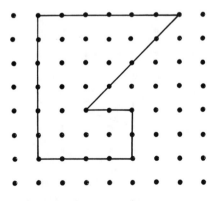

Each side of figure B has been _____ to

_____ times as long.

IDENTIFYING ENLARGEMENT AND REDUCTION

Compare figure B to figure A. Decide whether figure B has been enlarged or reduced and by what factor.

A-145

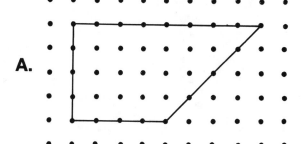

A.

B.

Each side of figure B has been _____ to _____ times as long.

A-146

A.

B.

Each side of figure B has been _____ to _____ times as long.

A-147

A.

B.

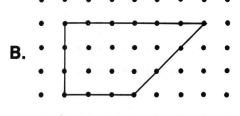

Each side of figure B has been _____ to _____ times as long.

© 1985 MIDWEST PUBLICATIONS 93950

USING LARGER GRIDS TO ENLARGE FIGURES

You have practiced enlarging figures by multiplying the length of sides by an enlargement factor. For this activity you used a grid having the same units.

You can also enlarge a figure by drawing the figure on the corresponding dots of a grid having units twice as large.

Enlarge the figure below by matching points on the small grid with points on the large grid.

EXAMPLE:

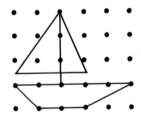

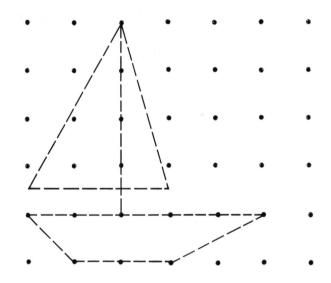

A-148

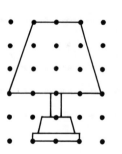

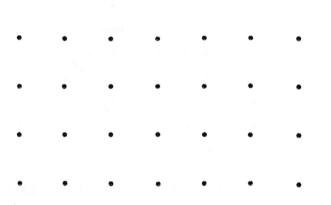

USING LARGER GRIDS TO ENLARGE FIGURES

Enlarge each figure by matching points on the small grid with points on the large grid.

A-149

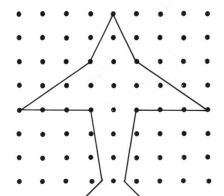

A-150

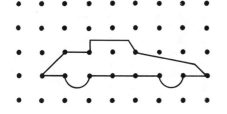

USING SMALLER GRIDS TO REDUCE FIGURES

Reduce the figure by matching points on the large grid with points on the small grid.

EXAMPLE:

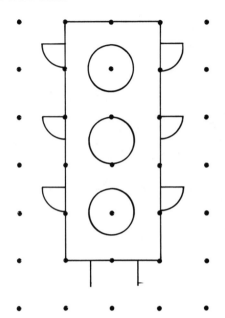

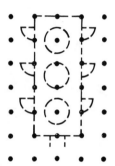

A-151

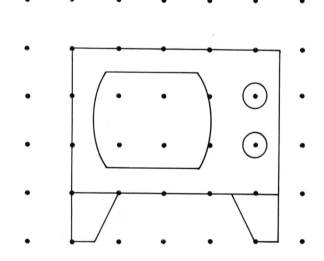

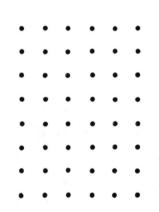

© 1985 MIDWEST PUBLICATIONS 93950

USING SMALLER GRIDS TO REDUCE FIGURES

Reduce the figures by matching points on the large grid with points on the small grid.

A-152

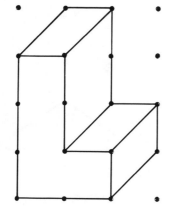

A-153

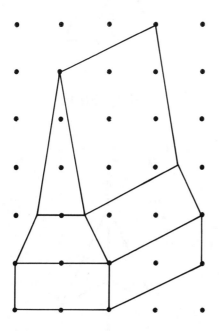

SIMILARITIES

RECOGNIZING LINES OF SYMMETRY

A figure has a **line of symmetry** if it can be folded so that the two sides are congruent (exactly alike). Examine these figures and circle **yes** if the arrow is a line of symmetry, or **no** if it is not.

A-154

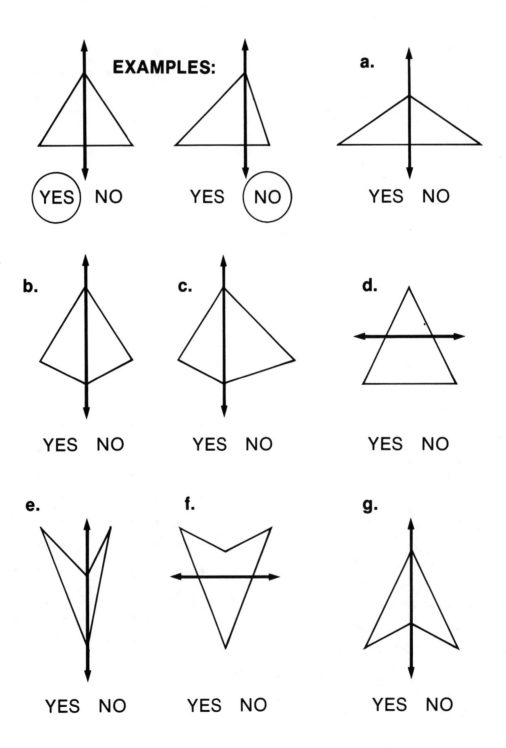

EXAMPLES:

YES NO

a.

YES NO

YES NO

b.
YES NO

c.
YES NO

d.
YES NO

e.
YES NO

f.
YES NO

g.
YES NO

RECOGNIZING LINES OF SYMMETRY

A figure has a **line of symmetry** if it can be folded so that the two sides are congruent (exactly alike). Examine these figures and circle **yes** if the arrow is a line of symmetry, or **no** if it is not.

A-155

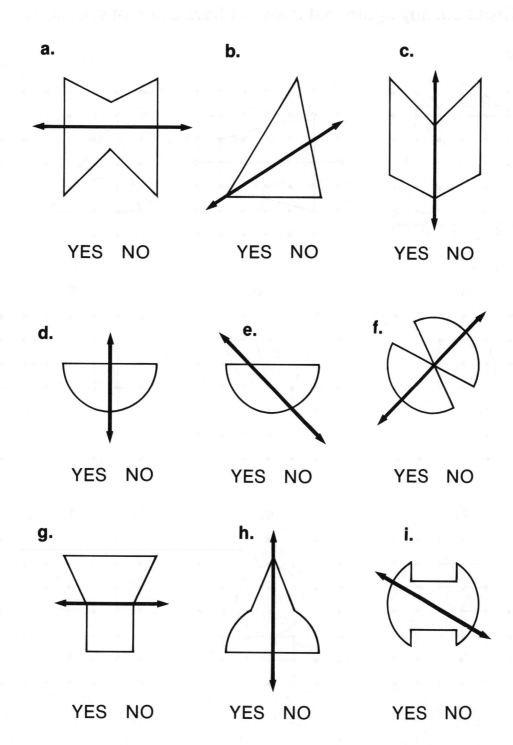

a.

YES　NO

b.

YES　NO

c.

YES　NO

d.

YES　NO

e.

YES　NO

f.

YES　NO

g.

YES　NO

h.

YES　NO

i.

YES　NO

DRAWING LINES OF SYMMETRY

Divide these figures into symmetrical (congruent) parts. If the figure has been divided correctly, corresponding points on either side of the figure should be the same distance from the line of symmetry. Count the dots to be sure that the line of symmetry is in the correct position.

Cross out any figure that does not have a line of symmetry.

EXAMPLES:

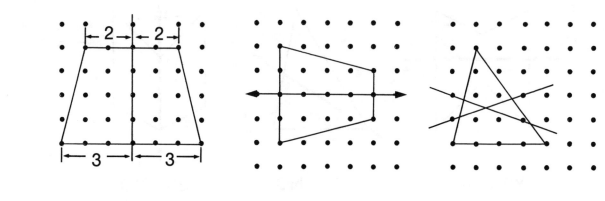

A-156

a.	b.	c.

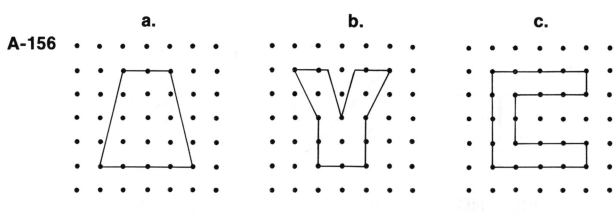

d.	e.	f.

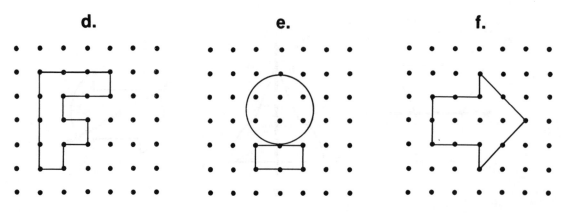

DRAWING LINES OF SYMMETRY

Divide these figures into symmetrical (congruent) parts. If the figure has been divided correctly, corresponding points on either side of the figure should be the same distance from the line of symmetry. Count the dots to be sure that the line of symmetry is in the correct position.

Cross out any figure that does not have a line of symmetry.

A-157

a.

b.

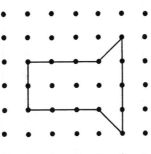

c.

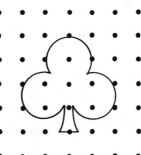

d.

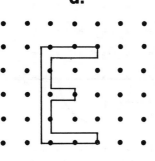

e.

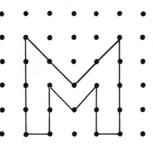

f.

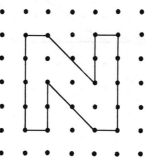

g.

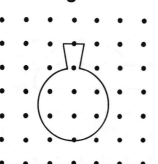

h.

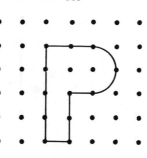

i.

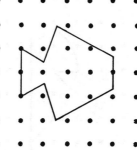

PRODUCING SYMMETRICAL FIGURES

In the last exercise, you could test for symmetry by counting an equal number of dots on each side of the line of symmetry. Use the same principle to draw the symmetrical (congruent) half of each of these figures.

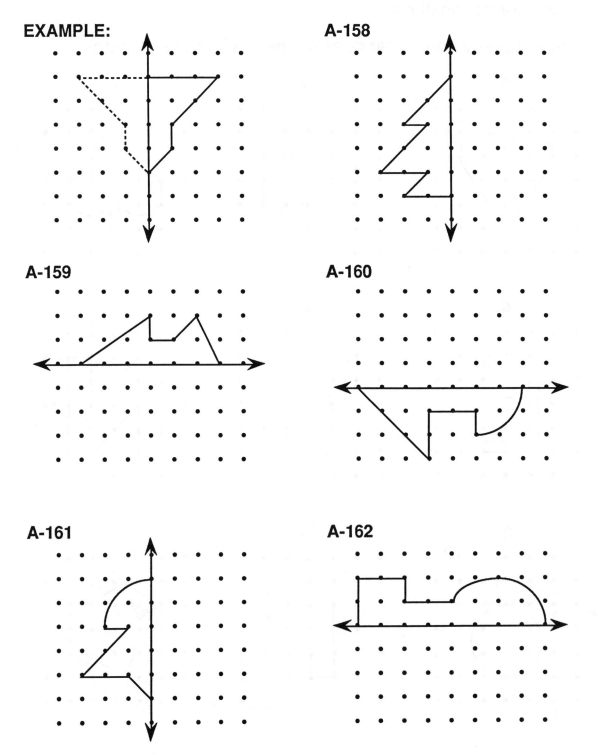

EXAMPLE:

A-158

A-159

A-160

A-161

A-162

PRODUCING SYMMETRICAL FIGURES

In the last exercise, you could test for symmetry by counting an equal number of dots on each side of the line of symmetry. Use the same principle to draw the symmetrical (congruent) half of each of these figures.

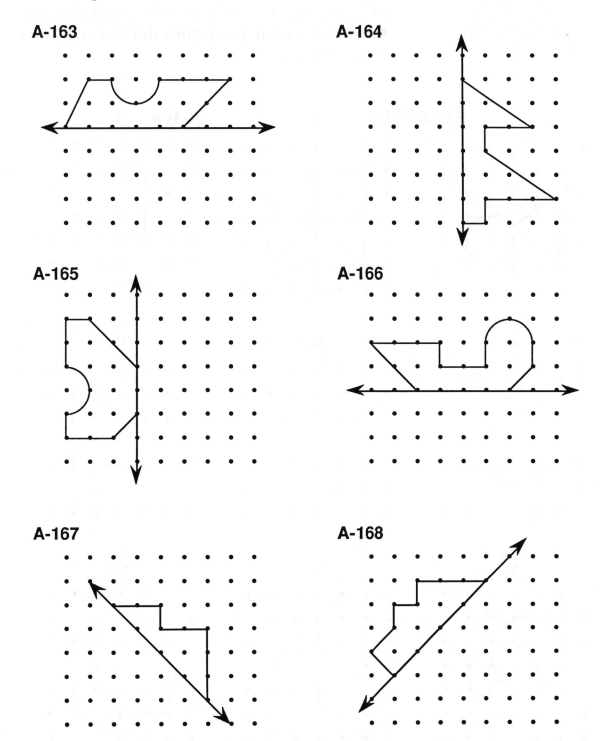

A-163

A-164

A-165

A-166

A-167

A-168

DRAWING MULTIPLE LINES OF SYMMETRY

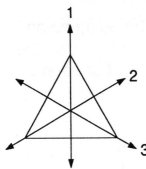

Figures can have more than one line of symmetry. An equilateral triangle has three.

On the following figures, draw all the lines of symmetry that you can find. Number the lines. Cross out any figure that has no lines of symmetry.

EXAMPLES: **A-169**   **a.**

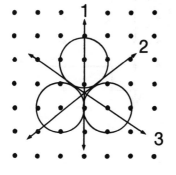

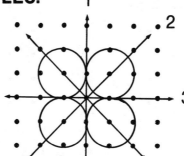

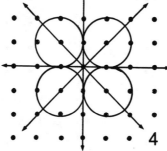

b.   **c.**   **d.**

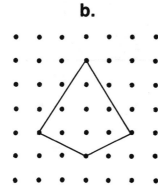

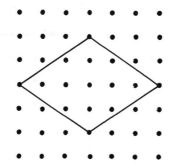

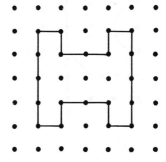

e.   **f.**   **g.**

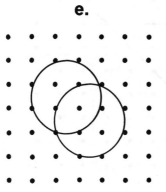

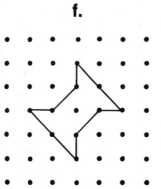

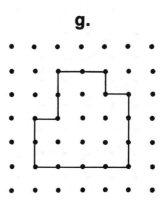

DRAWING MULTIPLE LINES OF SYMMETRY

Draw all the lines of symmetry that you can find on the figures below. Number the lines. Cross out any figure that has no line of symmetry.

A-170

a.

b.

c.

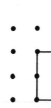
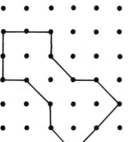
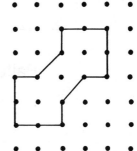

d.

e.

f.

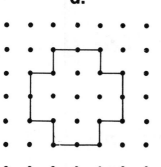
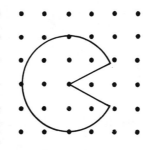
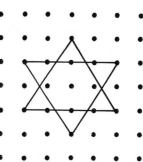

g.

h.

i.

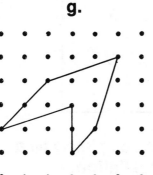
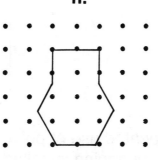
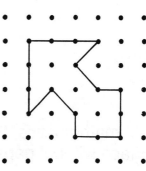

COVERING A SURFACE

Draw the pattern on the dot grid as many times as needed to cover the whole grid. There should be **no** empty space left in the grid and **no** overlapping shapes.

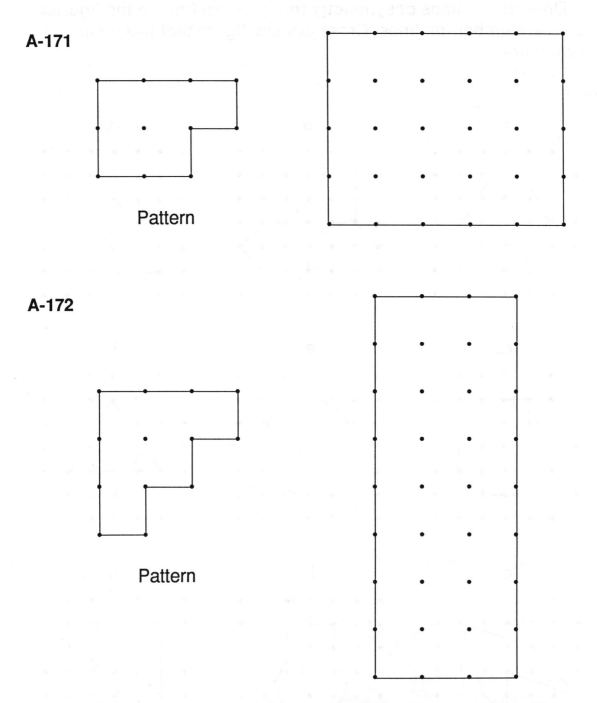

A-171

Pattern

A-172

Pattern

In mathematics, the repeated use of polygons to completely fill a surface without gaps or overlapping is called a **tessellation.**

COVERING A SURFACE

Draw the pattern on the dot grid as many times as needed to cover the whole grid. There should be **no** empty space left in the grid and **no** overlapping. This process is called a **tessellation.**

SIMILARITIES

A-173

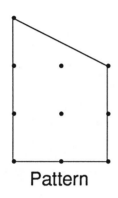

Pattern

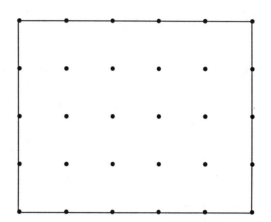

A-174

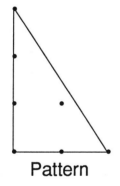

Pattern

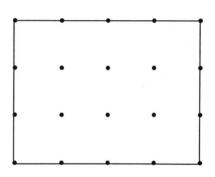

A-175

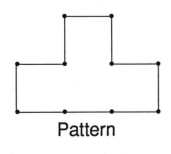

Pattern

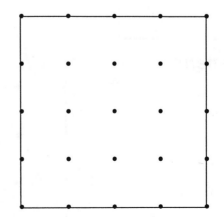

COVERING A SURFACE

Draw the pattern on the dot grid as many times as needed to cover the whole grid. There should be **no** empty space left in the grid and **no** overlapping shapes.

A-176

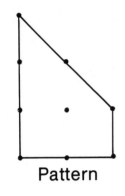

Pattern

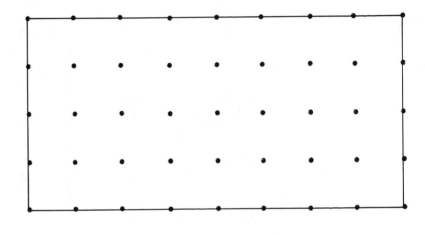

A-177

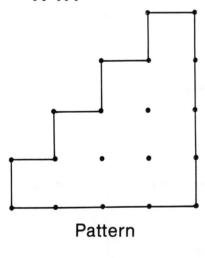

Pattern

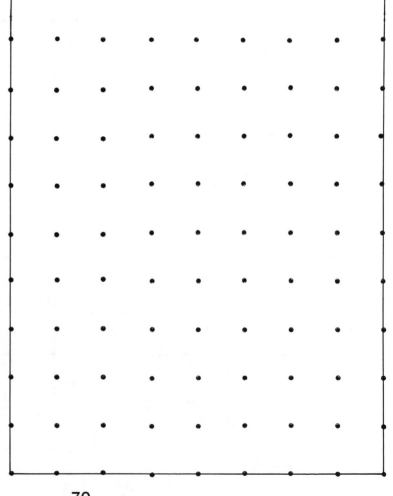

PRODUCING SIMILAR FIGURES BY TESSELLATION

Some shapes can be repeated (tessellated) to form a larger pattern of the **same** shape. Some cannot. Draw the larger pattern that can be made by tessellating the following shapes. Cross out any shape that cannot be tessellated to form a similar pattern.

EXAMPLE:

This small equilateral triangle can be tessellated to form this similar equilateral triangle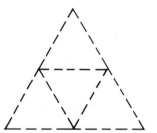

A-178

A-179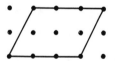

A-180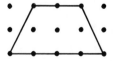

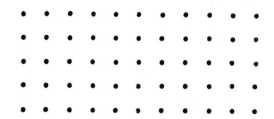

PRODUCING SIMILAR FIGURES BY TESSELLATION

Draw the larger pattern that can be made by tessellating the following shapes. Cross out any shapes that cannot be tessellated to form a similar pattern.

A-181

A-182

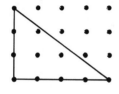

A-183

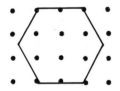

A-184

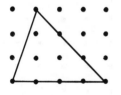

DRAWING TESSELLATING PATTERNS

Some figures can be filled by tessellating (repeating) shapes. Determine whether the following shapes will tessellate to form a hexagon.

A-185 Is it possible to fill a hexagon with equilateral triangles?

Yes_____ No_____

If so, draw the tessellation and tell how many triangles are needed to fill it.

How many? _____

If not, explain why not.

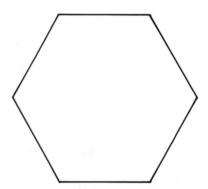

A-186 Is it possible to fill a hexagon with right triangles?

Yes_____ No_____

If so, draw the tessellation and tell how many triangles are needed to fill it.
How many? _____

If not, explain why not.

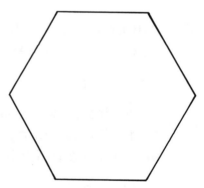

DRAWING TESSELLATING PATTERNS

Some figures can be filled by tessellating shapes. Determine whether the following shapes will tessellate to form a hexagon.

A-187 Is it possible to fill a hexagon with diamond shaped figures?

Yes____ No____

If so, draw the tessellation and tell how many diamond shapes are needed to fill it.

How many? _____

If not, explain why not.

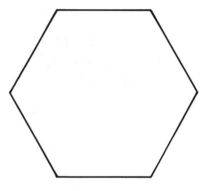

A-188 Is it possible to fill a hexagon with squares?

Yes____ No____

If so, draw the tessellation and tell how many squares are needed to fill it.

How many? _____

If not, explain why not.

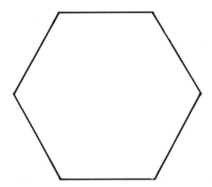

A-189 Is it possible to fill a hexagon with hexagons?

Yes____ No____

If so, draw the tessellation and tell how many hexagons are needed to fill it.

How many? _____

If not, explain why not.

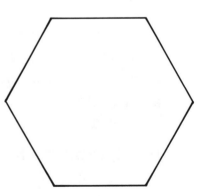

© 1985 MIDWEST PUBLICATIONS 93950

POLYOMINOES

Polyominoes are formed by congruent squares placed next to each other so that their entire sides coincide.

NUMBER	NAME	EXAMPLES
1	Monomino	
2	Domino	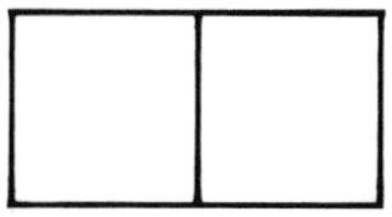
3	Trominoes	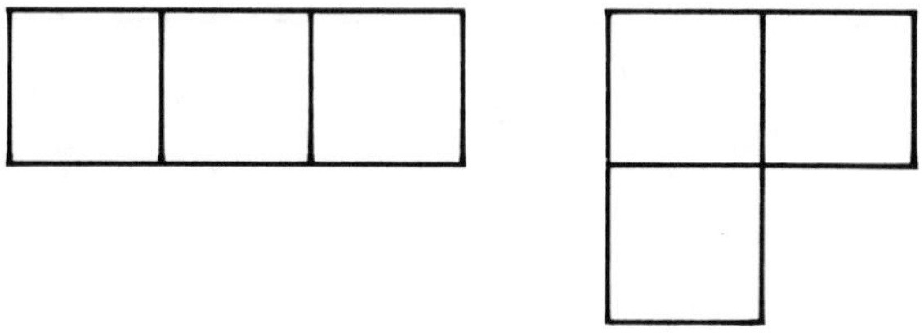
4	Tetrominoes	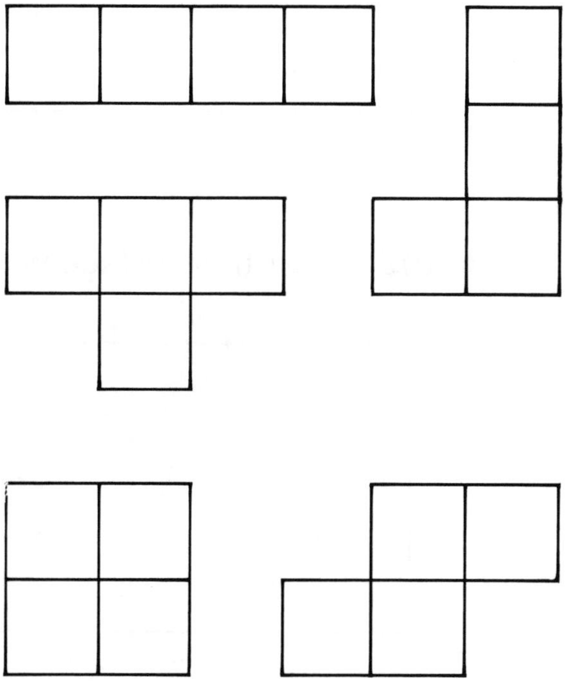

POLYOMINOES

A-190 Cover this surface with two pair of trominoes.

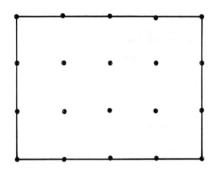

A-191 Cover this surface with three **different** pair of tetrominoes.

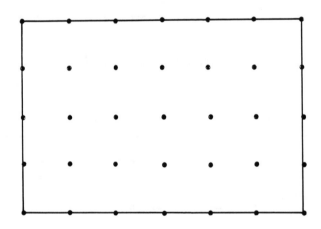

A-192 Cover this surface with three **different** pair of tetrominoes.

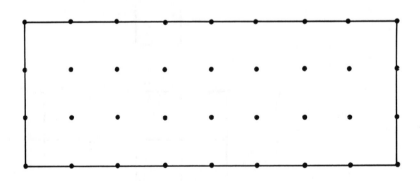

© 1985 MIDWEST PUBLICATIONS 93950

POLYOMINOES

Pentominoes are patterns of **five** congruent squares placed next to each other so that their entire sides coincide.

EXAMPLE:

A-193 On the dot grid below, draw as many **different** pentomino patterns as you can form.

How many different pentomino patterns can you form?

POLYOMINOES

A-194 Cover this surface with any combination of pentominoes. Try to use as many different pentominoes as you can.

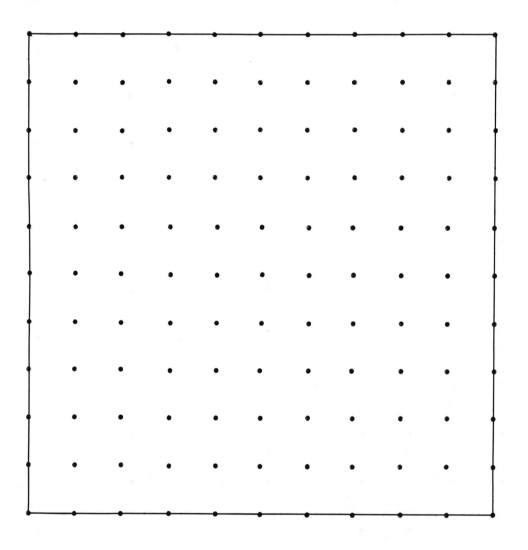

HOW MANY CUBES MAKE UP THE SOLID?

On the blank beside each solid, write the number of cubes that make up the solid.

EXAMPLE:　　　　　　　　**A-195**

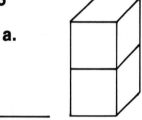
a.

_____

_2___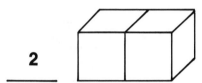

b.

_____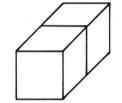

c.

_____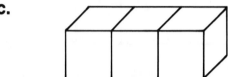

d.

_____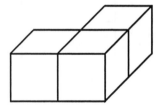

e.

_____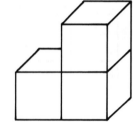

f.

_____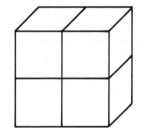

g.

_____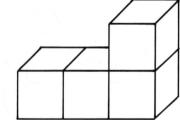

h.

_____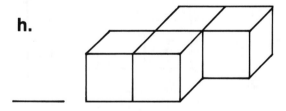

i.

_____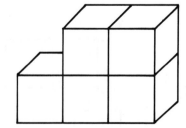

HOW MANY CUBES MAKE UP THE SOLID?

Write the number of cubes that make up each solid.

A-196

a.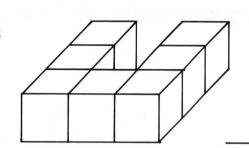

_____

b.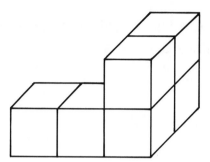

_____

c.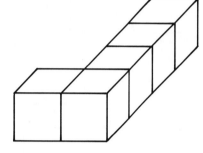

_____

d.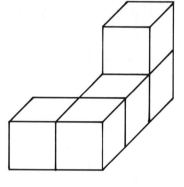

_____

e.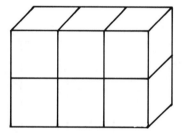

_____

f.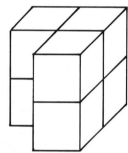

_____

g.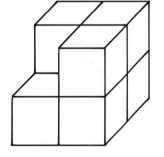

_____

h.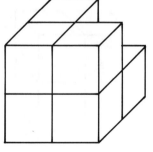

_____

i.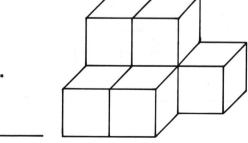

_____

j.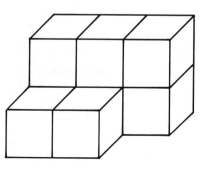

_____

MATCHING VOLUME

Draw a line from each solid on the left to a solid on the right that contains the same number of cubes. Shapes that contain the same number of cubes have the same volume.

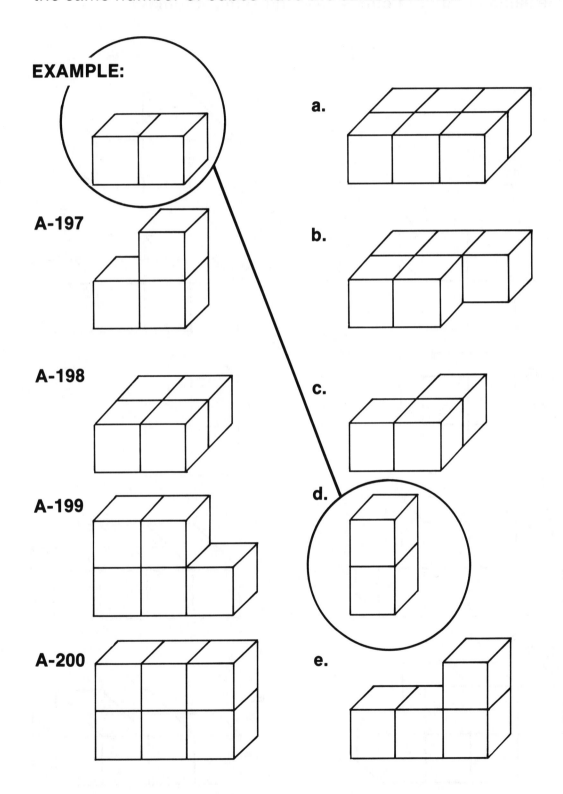

EXAMPLE:

A-197

A-198

A-199

A-200

a.

b.

c.

d.

e.

MATCHING VOLUME

Draw a line from each solid on the left to a solid on the right
that contains the same number of cubes. Shapes that contain
the same number of cubes have the same volume.

A-201

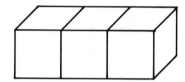

a.

A-202

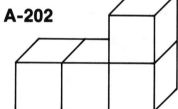

b.

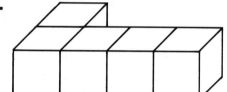

A-203

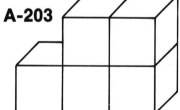

c.

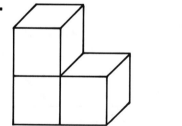

A-204

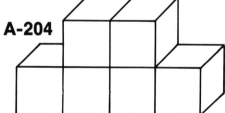

d.

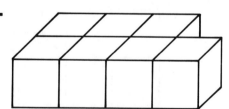

A-205

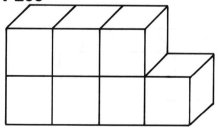

e.

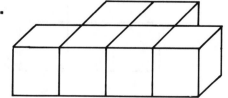

RECOGNIZING VOLUME

Decide how many of the solids on the left are contained in the solid on the right.

A-206

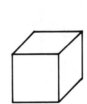 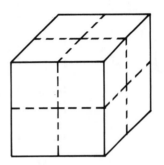

Number of solids on the top row ____

Number of solids on the bottom row ____

Total number ____

A-207

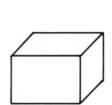 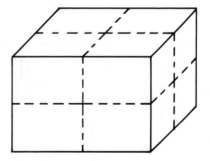

Number of solids on the top row ____

Number of solids on the bottom row ____

Total number ____

SIMILARITIES

RECOGNIZING VOLUME

Decide how many of the solids on the left are contained in the solid on the right.

A-208

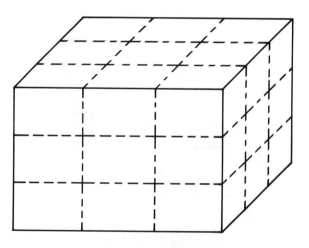

Number of solids on the top row _____

Number of solids in the middle row _____

Number of solids on the bottom row _____

Total number _____

A-209

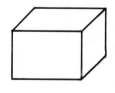

Number of solids on the top row _____

Number of solids in the middle row _____

Number of solids on the bottom row _____

Total number _____

RECOGNIZING VOLUME

Decide how many of the solids on the left are contained in the solid on the right.

A-210

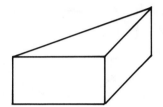

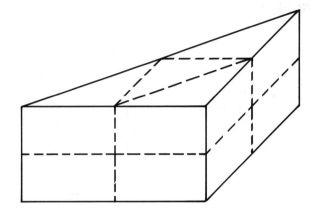

Number of solids on the top row _____

Number of solids on the bottom row _____

Total number _____

A-211

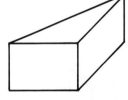

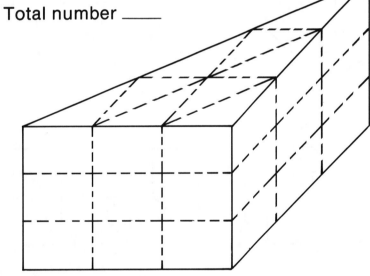

Number of solids on the top row _____

Number of solids in the middle row _____

Number of solids on the bottom row _____

Total number _____

IDENTIFYING CONGRUENT SOLIDS

In each row, circle the two solids that have the same size and shape. Such solids are congruent.

EXAMPLE:

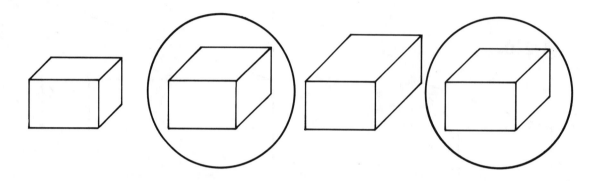

A-212   **a.**   **b.**   **c.**   **d.**

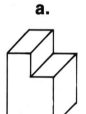 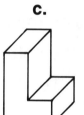 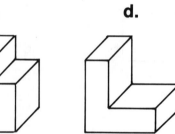

A-213   **a.**   **b.**   **c.**   **d.**

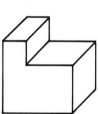 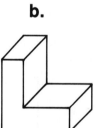

A-214   **a.**   **b.**   **c.**   **d.**

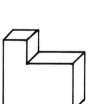 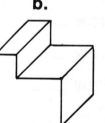 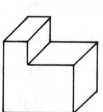 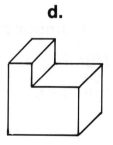

IDENTIFYING CONGRUENT SOLIDS

In each row, circle the solids that have the same size and shape. Such solids are congruent.

A-215 a. b. c. d.

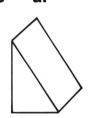 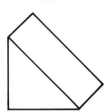 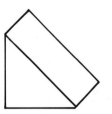 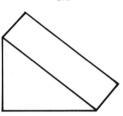

a. b. c. d.

A-216

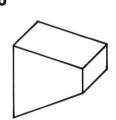 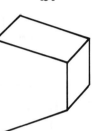 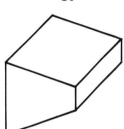 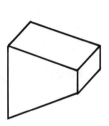

A-217 a. b. c. d.

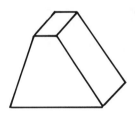  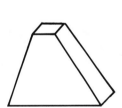 

A-218 a. b. c. d.

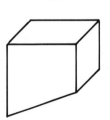 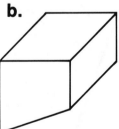 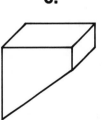 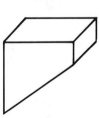

A-219 a. b. c. d.

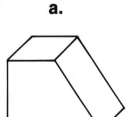 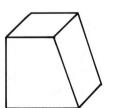 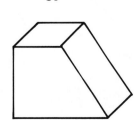 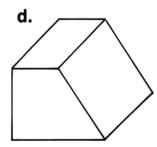

MATCHING CONGRUENT SOLIDS

Draw a line from each solid on the left to its congruent twin on the right.

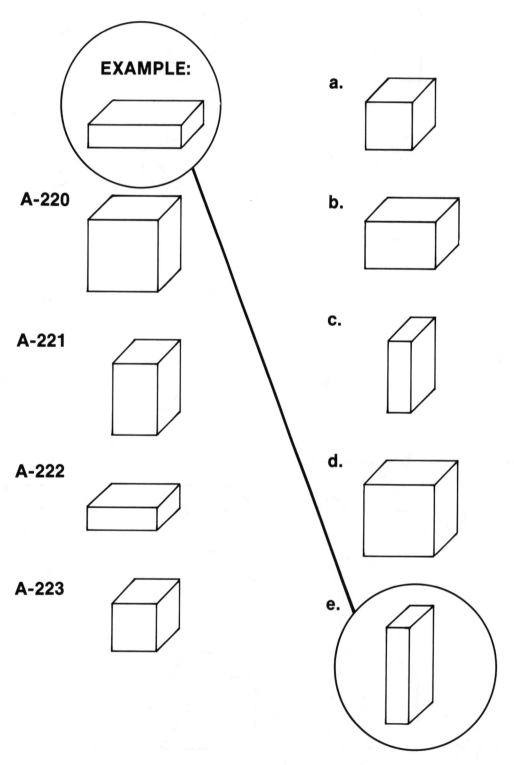

EXAMPLE:

a.

A-220

b.

A-221

c.

A-222

d.

A-223

e.

MATCHING CONGRUENT SOLIDS

Draw a line from each solid on the left to its congruent twin on the right.

A-224 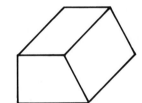   **a.**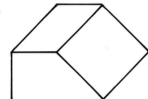

A-225 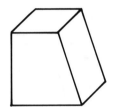   **b.**

A-226 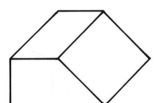   **c.**

A-227 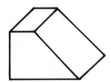   **d.**

MATCHING CONGRUENT SOLIDS

Draw a line from each solid on the left to its congruent twin on the right.

A-228 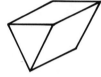   **a.**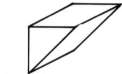

A-229    **b.**

A-230 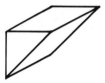   **c.**

A-231    **d.**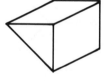

A-232    **e.**

RECOGNIZING VIEWS OF A SOLID

Imagine that you are drawing a pattern to cover each face of a solid.

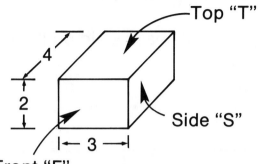

The top is 3 units by 4 units
The side is 2 units by 4 units
The front is 2 units by 3 units

Which group of pattern pieces fits each solid on the left?

EXAMPLE:

A-233

A-234

A-235

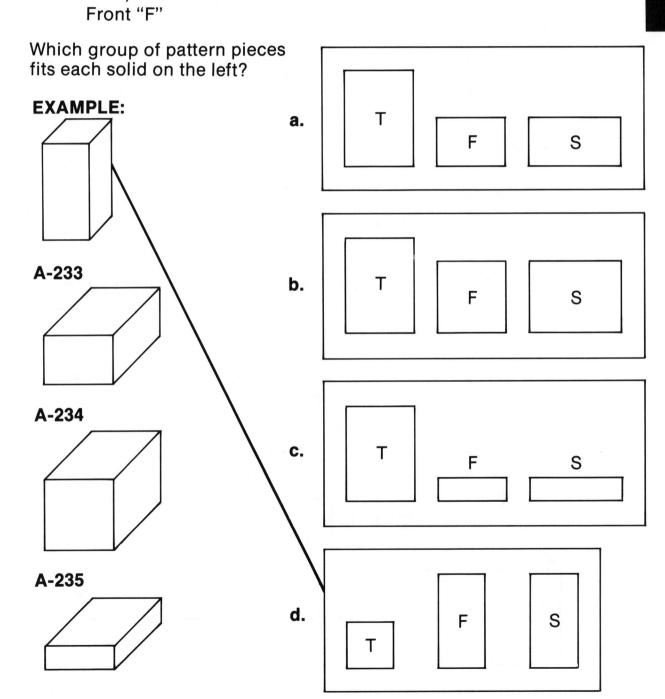

RECOGNIZING VIEWS OF A SOLID

Which group of pattern pieces fits each solid on the left?

A-236

a.

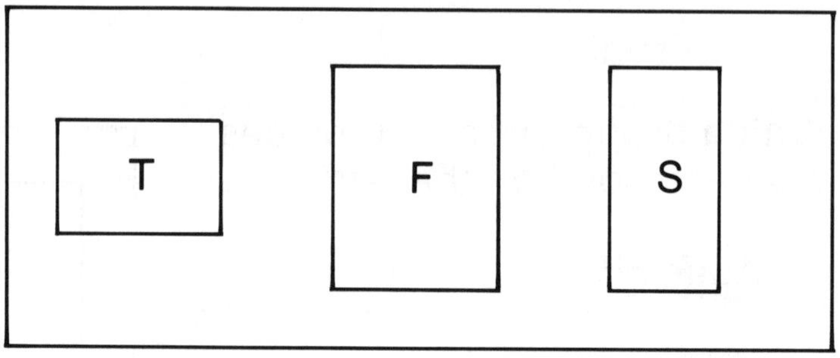

T	F	S

A-237

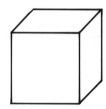

b.

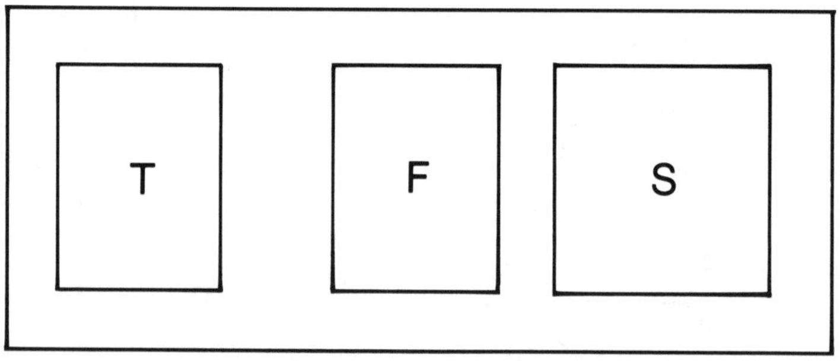

T	F	S

A-238

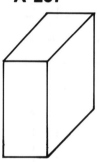

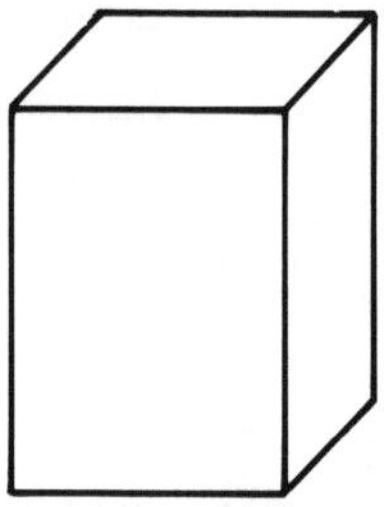

c.

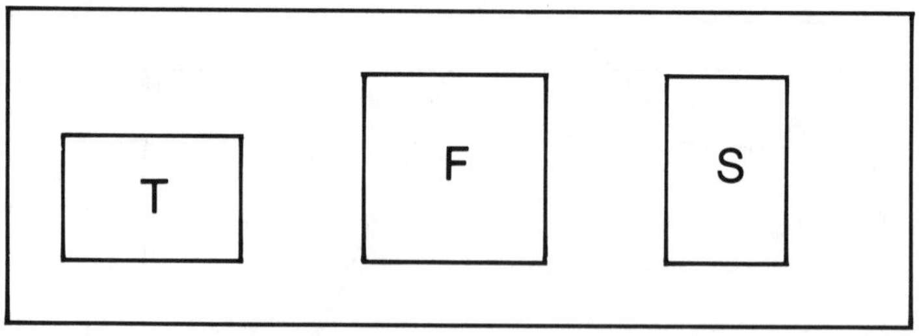

T	F	S

A-239

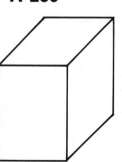

d.

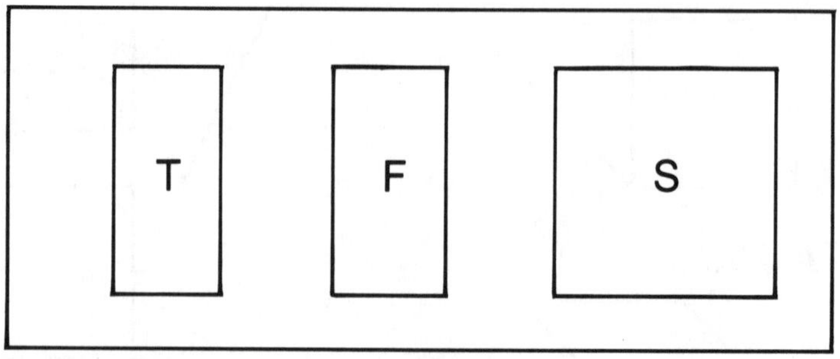

T	F	S

RECOGNIZING VIEWS OF A SOLID

Which group of pattern pieces fits each solid on the left?

A-240
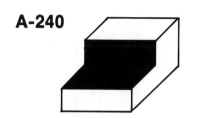

a.
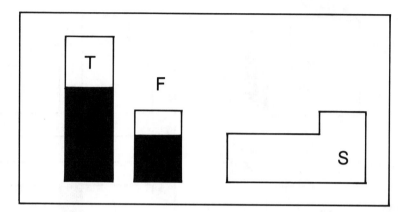

A-241
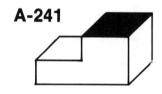

b.
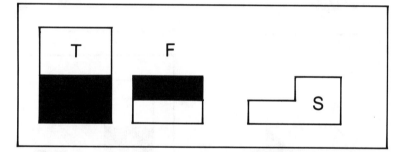

A-242
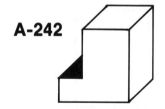

c.
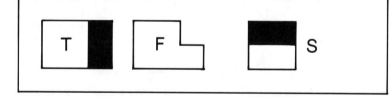

A-243
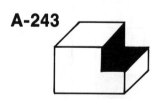

d.
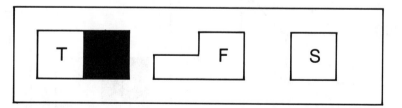

A-244
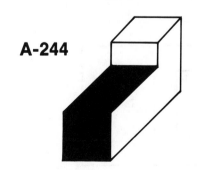

e.
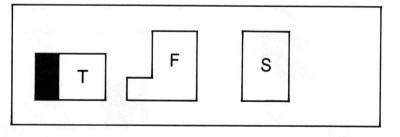

SIMILARITIES

RECOGNIZING VIEWS OF A SOLID

Which group of pattern pieces fits each solid on the left?

A-245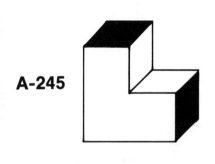

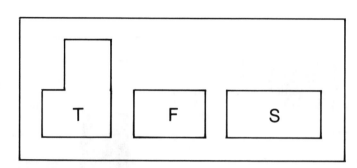

a.

A-246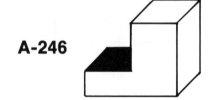

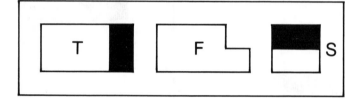

b.

A-247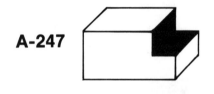

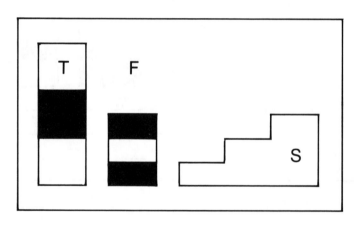

c.

A-248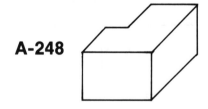

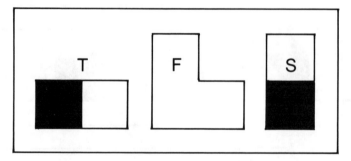

d.

A-249

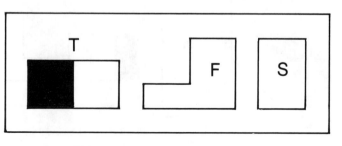

e.

COMBINING SOLIDS

Which two solids on the right form the solid on the left?

EXAMPLE:

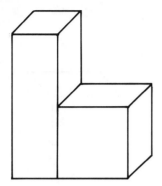

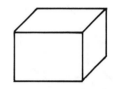
a.

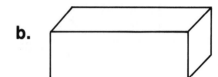
b.

Answer: __**b. + d.**__

A-250

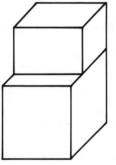

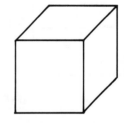
c.

Answer: _____

A-251

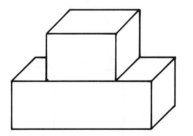

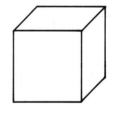
d.

Answer: _____

e.

A-252

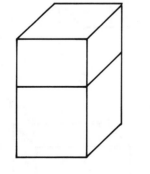

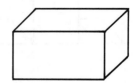
f.

Answer: _____

COMBINING SOLIDS

Which two solids on the right form the solid on the left?

A-253

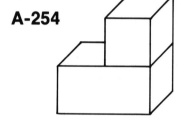

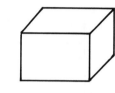

a.

Answer: _____

b.

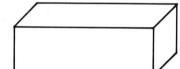

A-254

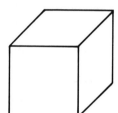

Answer: _____

c.

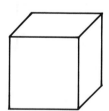

A-255

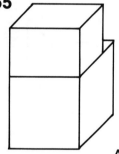

d.

Answer: _____

e.

A-256

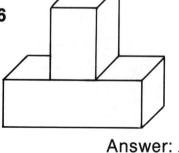

f.

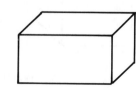

Answer: _____

COMBINING SOLIDS

Which two solids on the right form the solid on the left?

A-257

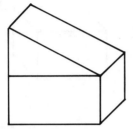

Answer: _____

a.

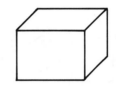

A-258

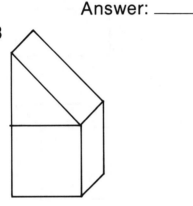

Answer: _____

b.

A-259

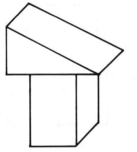

Answer: _____

c.

d.

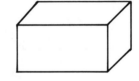

A-260

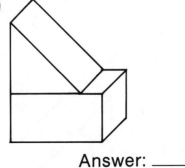

Answer: _____

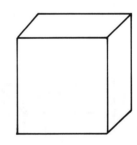

e.

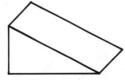

f.

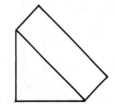

COMBINING SOLIDS

Which two solids on the right form the solid on the left?

A-261

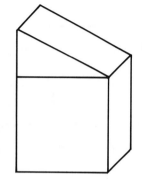

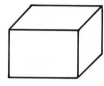

a.

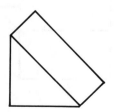

b.

Answer: _____

A-262

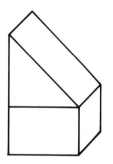

c.

Answer: _____

A-263

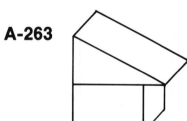

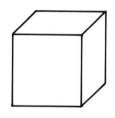

d.

Answer: _____

A-264

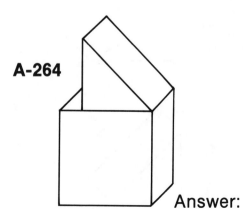

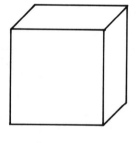

e.

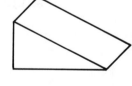

f.

Answer: _____

COMPLETE THE CUBE WITH ONE PIECE

Each cube has a piece missing. Circle the piece that will fill the cube.

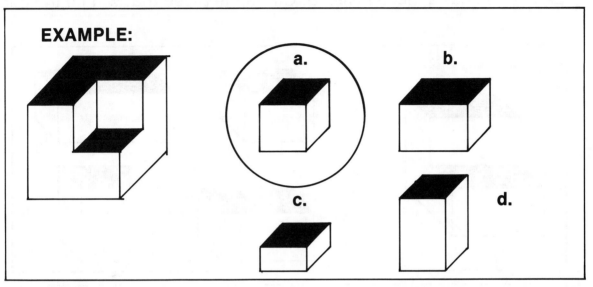

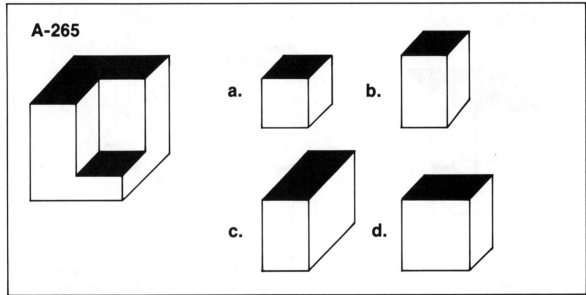

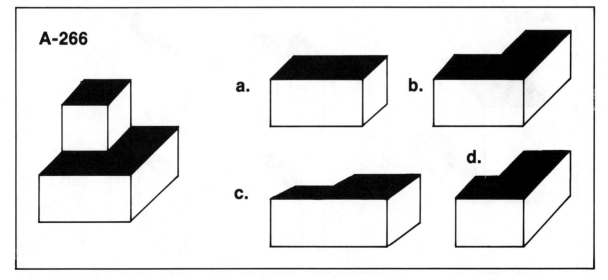

COMPLETE THE CUBE WITH ONE PIECE

Each cube has a piece missing. Circle the piece that will fill the cube.

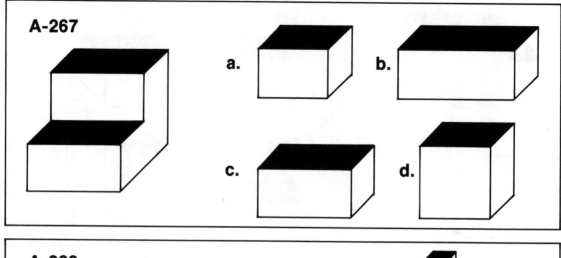

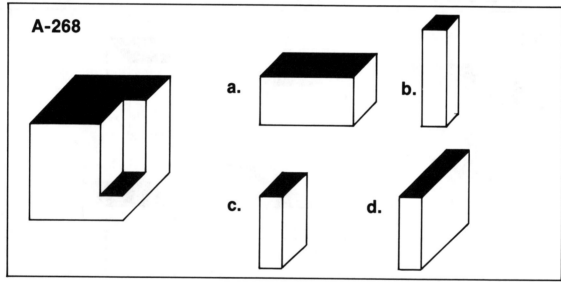

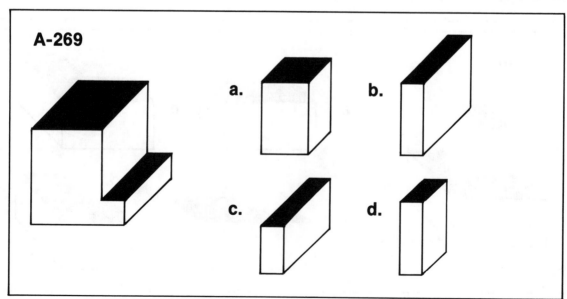

COMPLETE THE CUBE WITH ONE PIECE

Each cube has a piece missing. Circle the piece that will fill the cube.

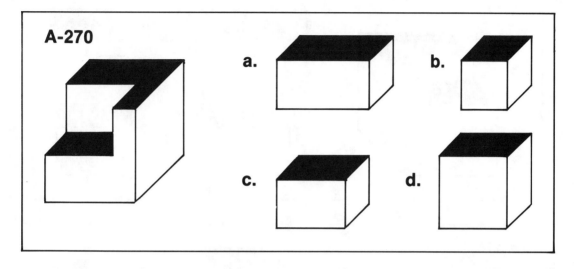

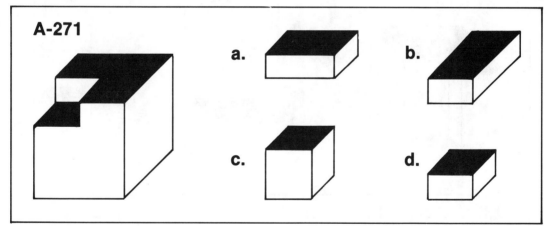

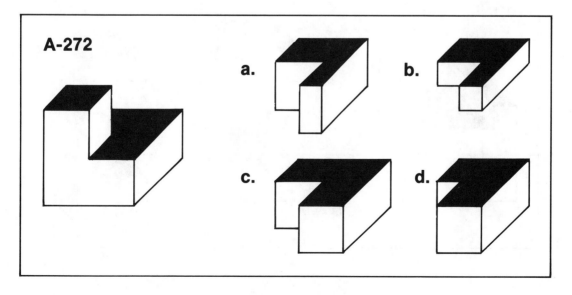

SIMILARITIES

COMPLETE THE CUBE WITH ONE PIECE

Each cube has a piece missing. Circle the piece that will fill the cube.

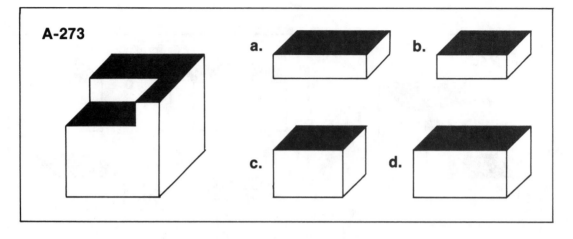

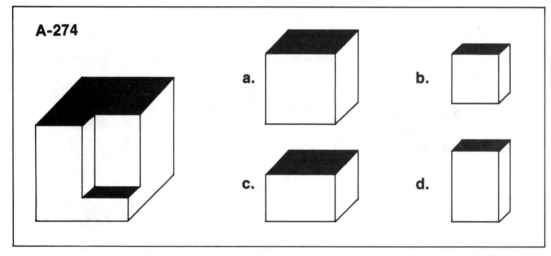

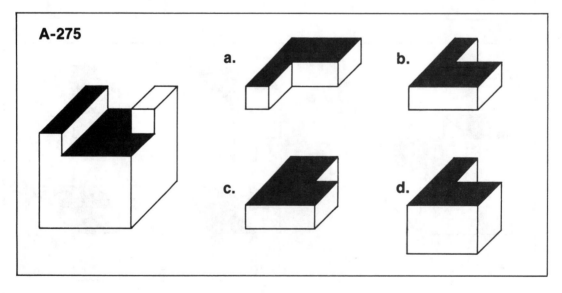

SEQUENCE OF FIGURES—SELECT

Examine the three figures in each row to determine a sequence of change. Select the figure from the choice box that continues the sequence. Write the letter for the next figure on the line.

EXAMPLE:

CHOICE BOX

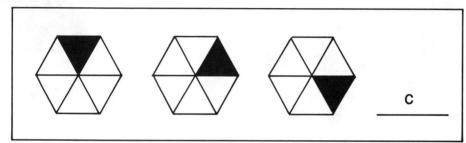   c

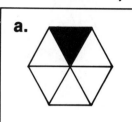 a.

B-1

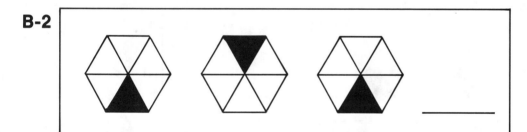 _____

 b.

B-2

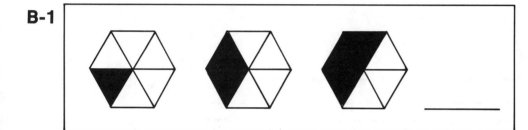 _____

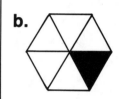 c.

B-3

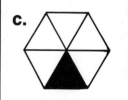 _____

 d.

B-4

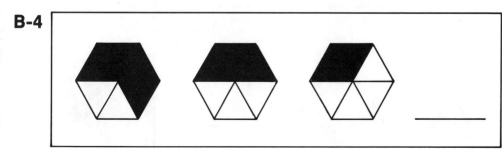 _____

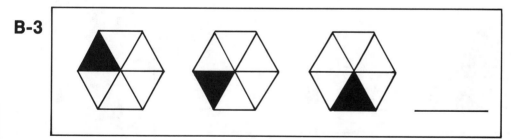 e.

 f.

SEQUENCES

SEQUENCE OF FIGURES—SELECT

Select the figure from the choice box that continues the
sequence. Write the letter for the next figure on the line.

CHOICE BOX

B-5

B-6

B-7

B-8

B-9

a.

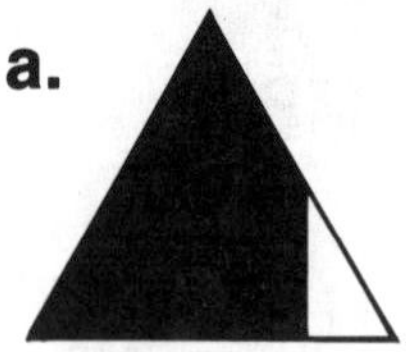

b.

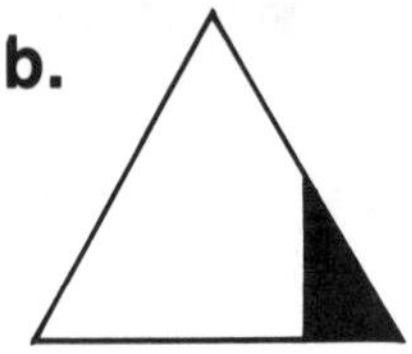

c.

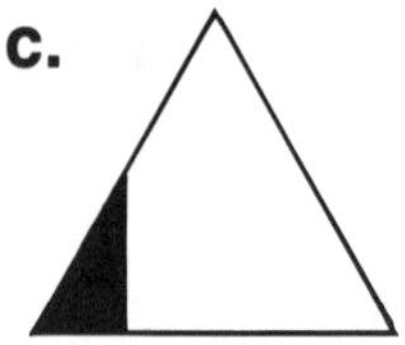

d.

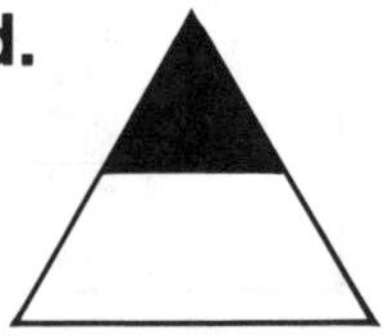

e.

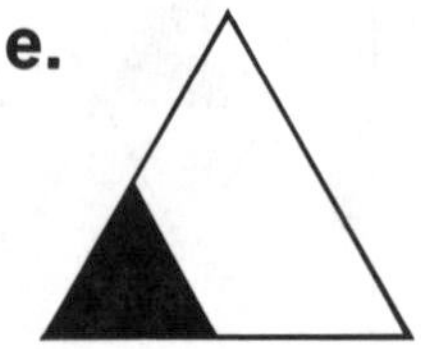

f.

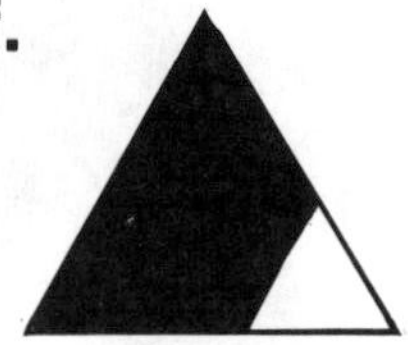

SEQUENCE OF FIGURES—SELECT

Select the figure from the choice box that continues the sequence. Write the letter for the next figure on the line.

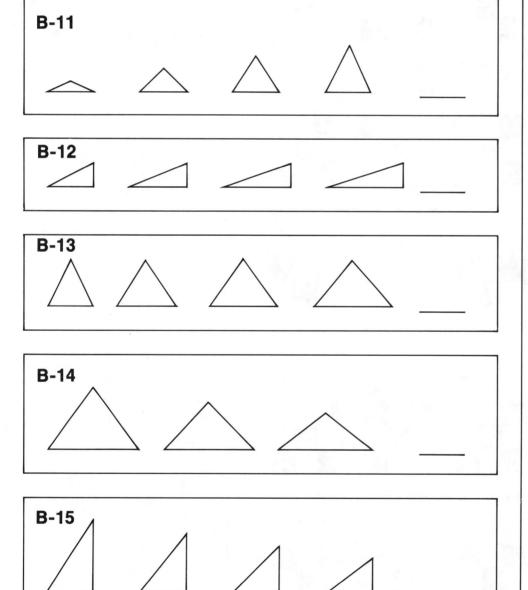

CHOICE BOX

 a.

 b.

 c.

 d.

 e.

f.

g.

h.

i.

SEQUENCES

SEQUENCE OF FIGURES—SUPPLY PATTERN

Draw the details in the fourth figure in each row as it should appear to continue each sequence.

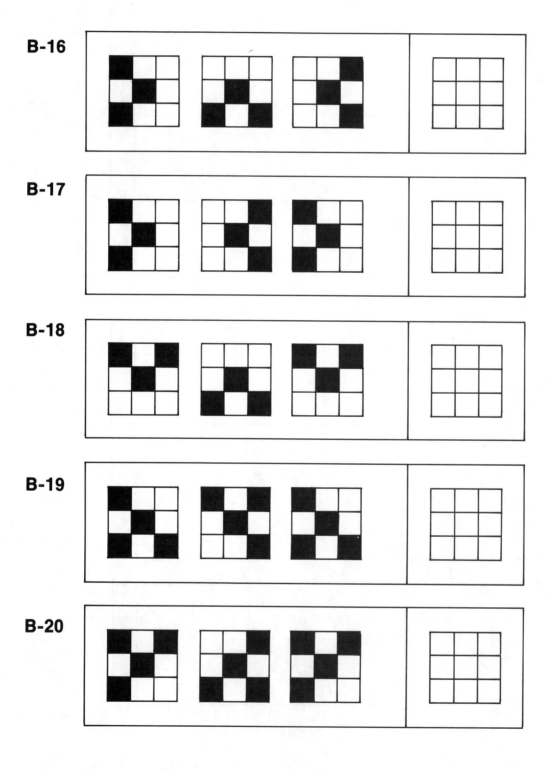

© 1985 MIDWEST PUBLICATIONS 93950

SEQUENCE OF FIGURES—SUPPLY PATTERN

Draw the details in the fourth figure in each row as it should appear to continue each sequence.

B-21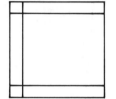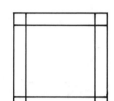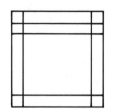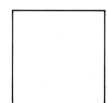

B-22

B-23

B-24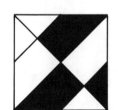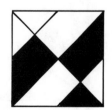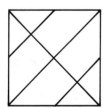

B-25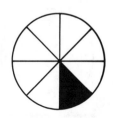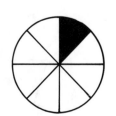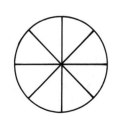

SEQUENCES

SEQUENCE OF FIGURES—SUPPLY PATTERN

Draw the details in the blank figure in each row as it should appear to continue the sequence.

	a.	**b.**	**c.**	**d.**

B-26

 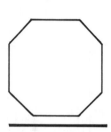 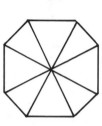

	a.	**b.**	**c.**	**d.**

B-27

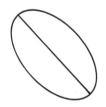   

	a.	**b.**	**c.**	**d.**

B-28

  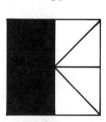 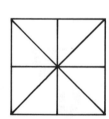

	a.	**b.**	**c.**	**d.**

B-29

 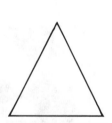 

	a.	**b.**	**c.**	**d.**

B-30

  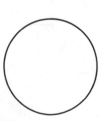 

SEQUENCE OF FIGURES—SUPPLY

Draw the fourth figure as it should appear to continue each sequence.

B-31

B-32

B-33

  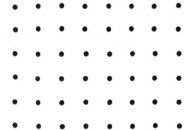

B-34

  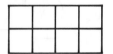 

B-35

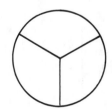 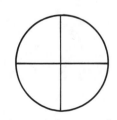 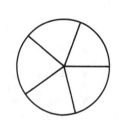 

SEQUENCES

SEQUENCE OF FIGURES—SUPPLY

On the grid, draw the group of figures that continues the sequence.

EXAMPLE:

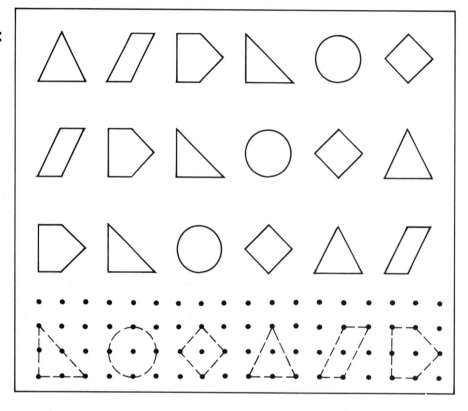

B-36

SEQUENCE OF FIGURES—SUPPLY

On the grid, draw the group of figures that continues the
sequence.

B-37

B-38

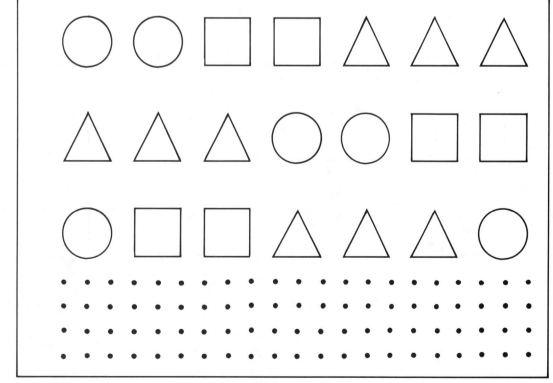

SEQUENCE OF FIGURES—SUPPLY

On the grid, draw the group of figures that continues the sequence.

B-39

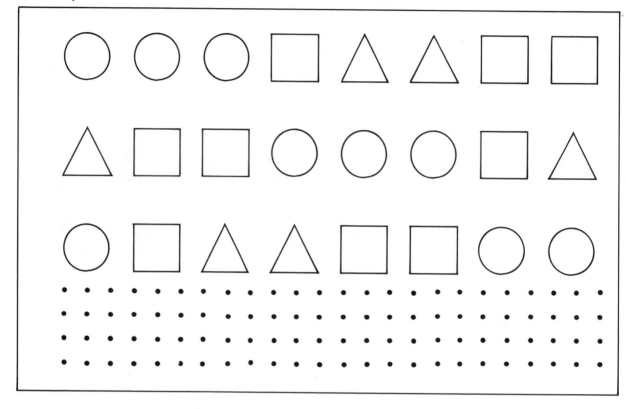

B-40

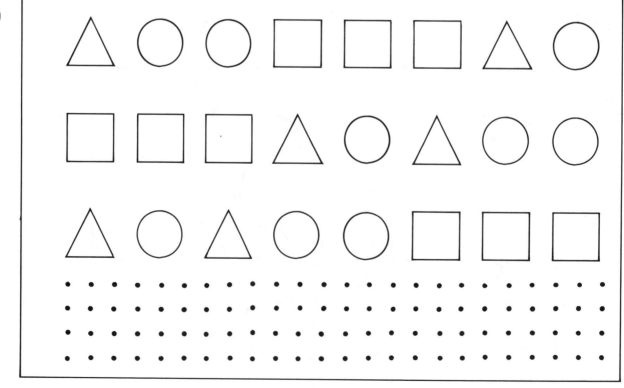

ROTATING FIGURES—FIND THE EXCEPTION

Turn each figure in the direction of the arrow. Cross out the figure in each row that you cannot get by rotating the first one.

EXAMPLE:

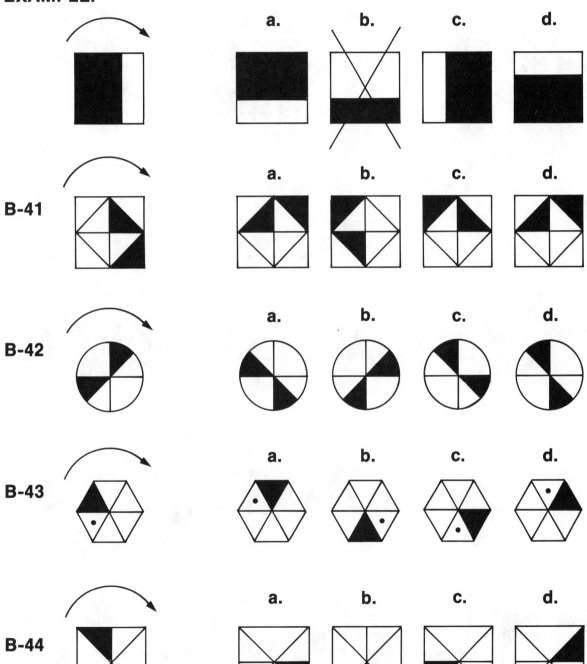

© 1985 MIDWEST PUBLICATIONS 93950

SEQUENCES

ROTATING FIGURES—FIND THE EXCEPTION

Turn each figure in the direction of the arrow. Cross out the figure in each row that you cannot get by rotating the first one.

B-45  a.  b.  c.  d.

B-46 a. b. c. d.

B-47 a. b. c. d.

B-48  a. 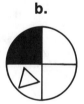 b. c.  d.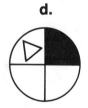

B-49  a. 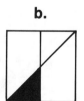 b. c.  d.

ROTATING FIGURES—SUPPLY

Draw each figure as it should appear after it has been rotated one position in the direction of the arrows.

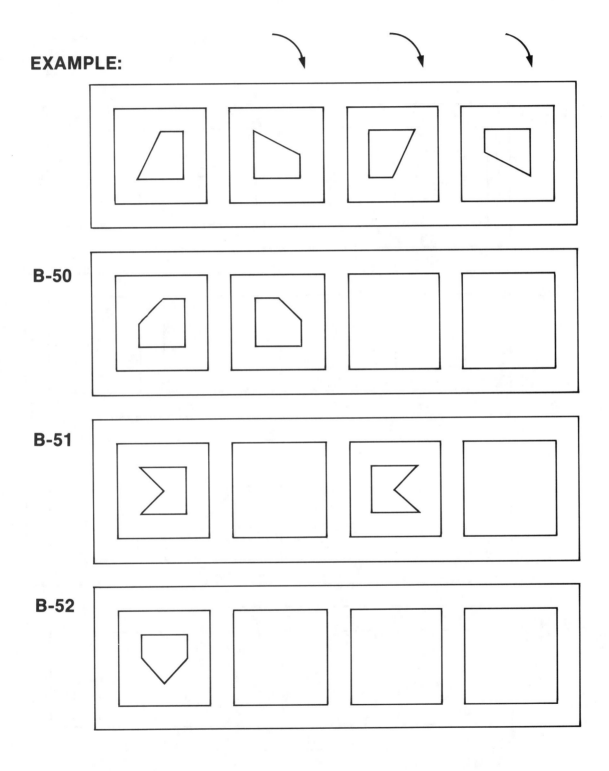

ROTATING FIGURES—SUPPLY

Draw each figure as it should appear after it has been rotated one position in the direction of the arrows.

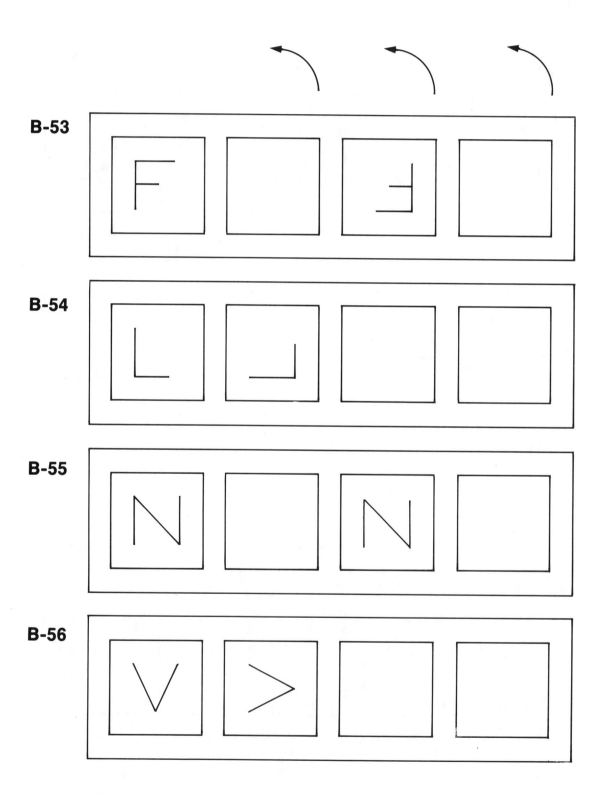

© 1985 MIDWEST PUBLICATIONS 93950

ROTATING FIGURES—SUPPLY

B-57   Draw how the hexagon will look when it has been rotated two positions to the left.

B-58   Draw how the hexagon will look when it has been rotated three positions to the right.

B-59   Draw how the hexagon will look when it has been rotated two positions to the right.

B-60   Draw how the hexagon will look when it has been rotated four positions to the left.

ROTATING FIGURES—EXPLAIN

How has figure "a" been rotated to produce figure "b"?

EXAMPLE:

a.　　　　　　**b.**

The square has been rotated
one position to the right.

a.　　　　　　**b.**

B-61　

_____

_____

a.　　　　　　**b.**

B-62　

_____

_____

a.　　　　　　**b.**

B-63　

_____

_____

a.　　　　　　**b.**

B-64　

_____

_____

ROTATING FIGURES—EXPLAIN

How has figure "a" been rotated to produce figure "b"?

B-65

a.　　b.

_____

_____

B-66

a.　　b.

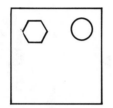

_____

_____

B-67

a.　　b.

_____

_____

B-68

a.　　b.

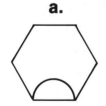

_____

_____

B-69

a.　　b.

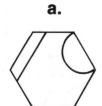

_____

_____

SEQUENCES

PRODUCING SINGLE REFLECTIONS

A reflection is the appearance of a figure after it has been flipped. The axis is the line along which it has been flipped. Draw what each figure will look like after it has been flipped along the axis indicated by the dotted line.

EXAMPLE:

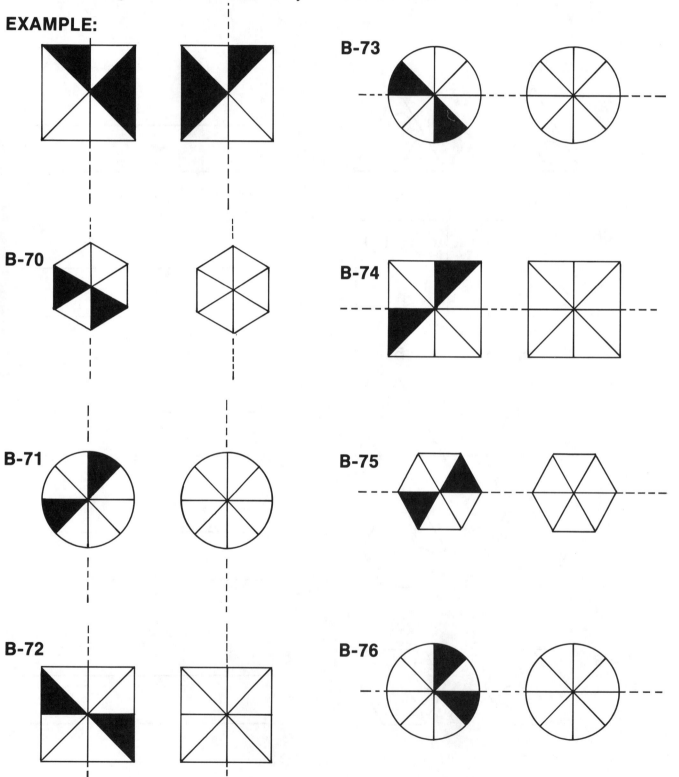

PRODUCING SINGLE REFLECTIONS

Draw what each figure will look like after it has been flipped along the axis indicated by the dotted line.

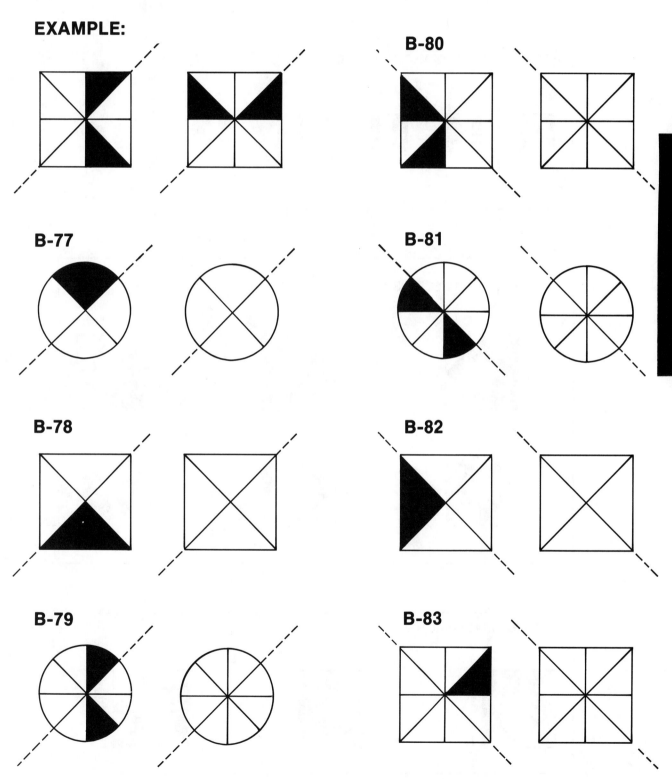

EXAMPLE:

B-80

B-77

B-81

B-78

B-82

B-79

B-83

SEQUENCES

MULTIPLE REFLECTIONS—SUPPLY

Figures may be reflected more than once along the vertical, horizontal, or diagonal axes.

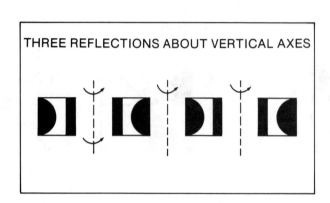

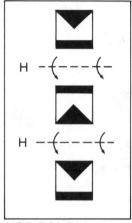

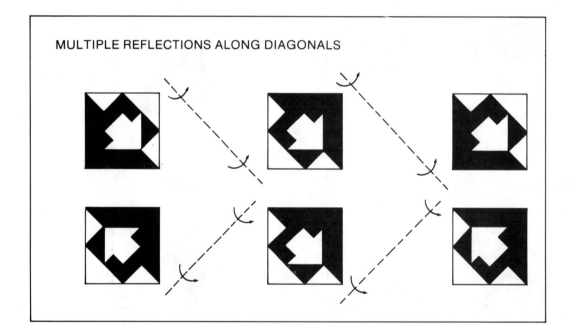

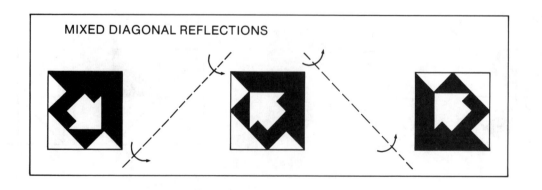

© 1985 MIDWEST PUBLICATIONS 93950

MULTIPLE REFLECTIONS—SUPPLY

Shade in each figure as it would appear after it has been
reflected along each axis in the indicated order.

B-84
  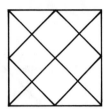  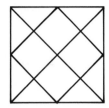

B-85
  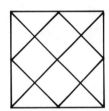  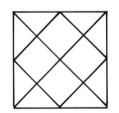

B-86
  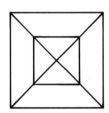  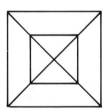

B-87
  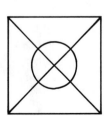  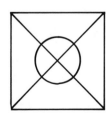

SEQUENCES

MULTIPLE REFLECTIONS—SUPPLY

Shade in each figure as it should appear after it has been reflected along each axis in the order indicated.

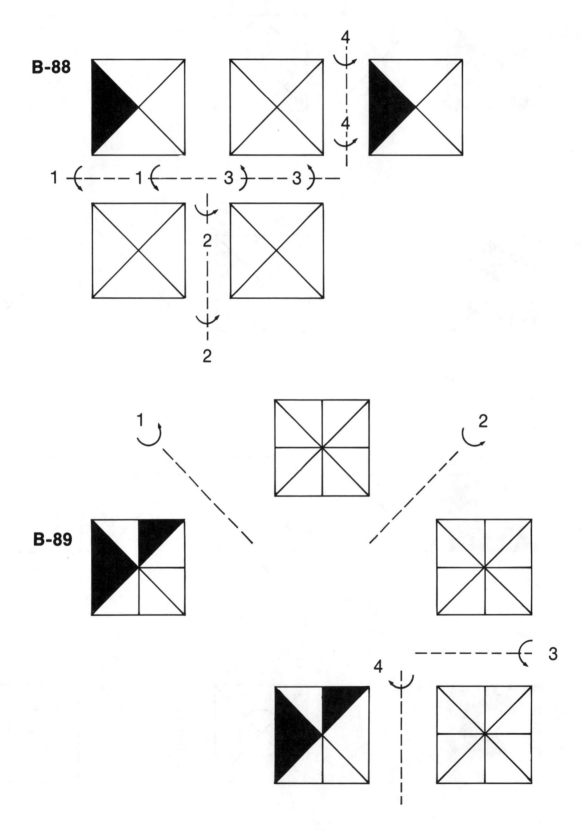

MULTIPLE REFLECTIONS—SUPPLY

Shade in each figure as it should appear after it has been reflected along each axis in the order indicated.

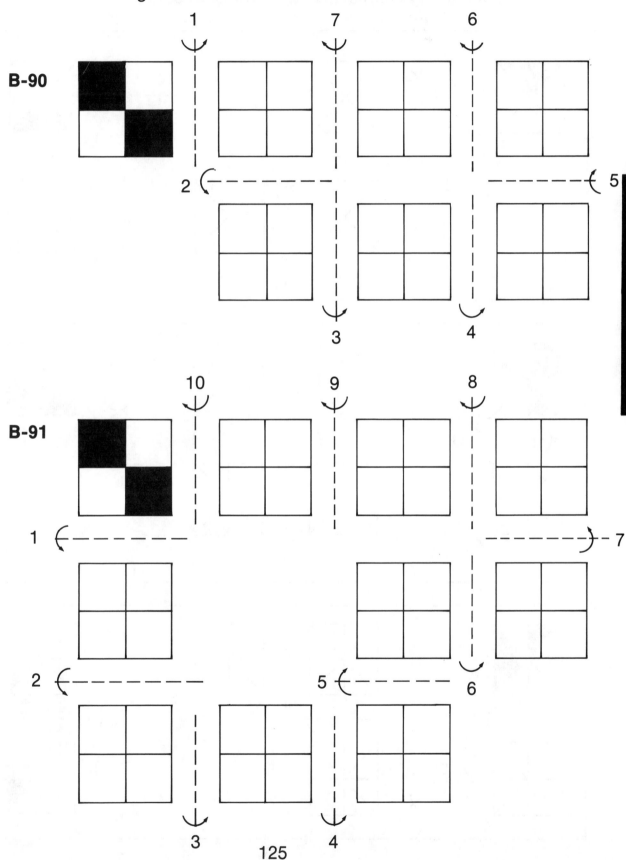

MULTIPLE REFLECTIONS—SUPPLY

Shade in each figure as it should appear after it has been reflected along each axis in the order indicated.

B-92

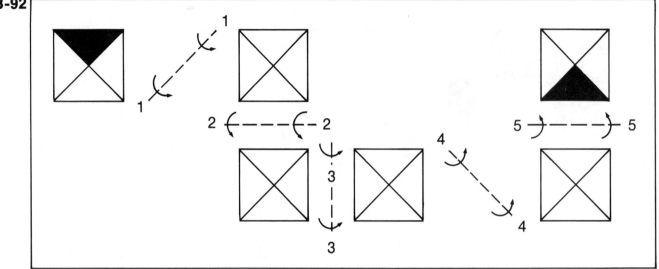

B-93

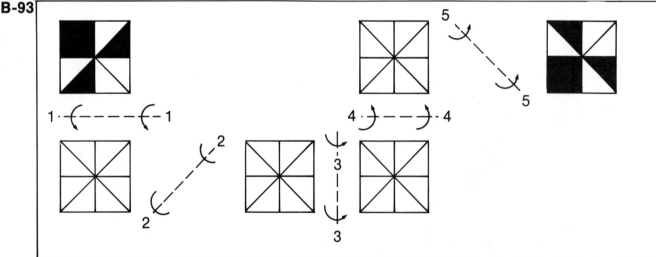

B-94

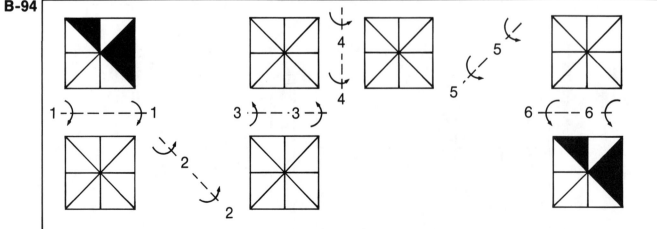

MULTIPLE REFLECTIONS—SUPPLY

Shade each figure as it should appear after it has been
reflected along each axis in the order indicated.

B-95

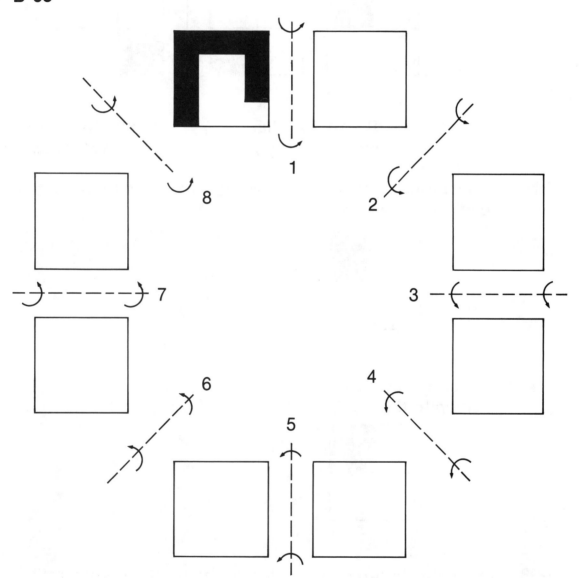

© 1985 MIDWEST PUBLICATIONS 93950

ROTATION AND REFLECTION—SUPPLY

Draw the figure that results from following the directions.

EXAMPLE: Rotate the figure one position to the right and then reflect it about the vertical axis.

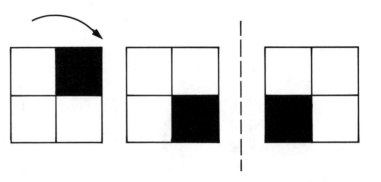

Step 1 (Do this
step mentally.)

Step 2 (This is the final
figure. You draw this.)

B-96 Reflect this figure about the vertical axis and then rotate it one position to the right.

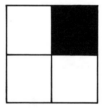

B-97 Reflect this figure about the horizontal axis and then rotate it one position to the right.

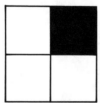

B-98 Rotate this figure one position to the right and then reflect it about the horizontal axis.

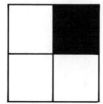

ROTATION AND REFLECTION—SUPPLY
Draw the figure that results from following the directions.

B-99 Rotate this figure two positions to the right and then reflect it about a vertical axis.

B-100 Reflect this figure about a vertical axis and then rotate it two positions to the right.

B-101 Reflect this figure about the diagonal ⟋ and then rotate it two positions to the left.

B-102 Rotate this figure two positions to the left and then reflect it about the ⟋ diagonal.

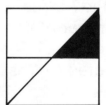

EXPLAINING ROTATION OR REFLECTION

Examine the figures below. Decide how the first figure has been rotated or reflected to make the second one. Mark the directions on the right to explain the change. Mark the axis **V** for vertical, **H** for horizontal, or **D** for diagonal.

B-103

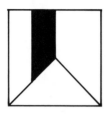 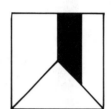

Rotated?   Yes_____ No_____
 Number of positions: _____
 Direction: Right_____ Left_____
Reflected?   Yes_____ No_____
 Axis: V_____ H_____ D_____

B-104

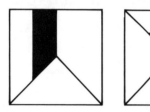

Rotated?   Yes_____ No_____
 Number of positions: _____
 Direction: Right_____ Left_____
Reflected?   Yes_____ No_____
 Axis: V_____ H_____ D_____

B-105

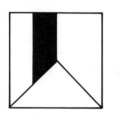

Rotated?   Yes_____ No_____
 Number of positions: _____
 Direction: Right_____ Left_____
Reflected?   Yes_____ No_____
 Axis: V_____ H_____ D_____

B-106

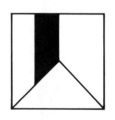 

Rotated?   Yes_____ No_____
 Number of positions: _____
 Direction: Right_____ Left_____
Reflected?   Yes_____ No_____
 Axis: V_____ H_____ D_____

B-107

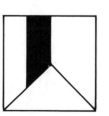 

Rotated?   Yes_____ No_____
 Number of positions: _____
 Direction: Right_____ Left_____
Reflected?   Yes_____ No_____
 Axis: V_____ H_____ D_____

EXPLAINING ROTATION OR REFLECTION

Mark the directions on the right to explain the change in the figures. Mark the axis **V** for vertical, **H** for horizontal, or **D** for diagonal.

B-108　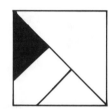

Rotated?　Yes＿＿　No＿＿
　　Number of positions: ＿＿
　　Direction:　Right＿＿　Left＿＿
Reflected?　Yes＿＿　　No＿＿
　　Axis:　V＿＿　H＿＿　D＿＿

B-109　

Rotated?　Yes＿＿　No＿＿
　　Number of positions: ＿＿
　　Direction:　Right＿＿　Left＿＿
Reflected?　Yes＿＿　　No＿＿
　　Axis:　V＿＿　H＿＿　D＿＿

B-110　

Rotated?　Yes＿＿　No＿＿
　　Number of positions: ＿＿
　　Direction:　Right＿＿　Left＿＿
Reflected?　Yes＿＿　　No＿＿
　　Axis:　V＿＿　H＿＿　D＿＿

B-111　

Rotated?　Yes＿＿　No＿＿
　　Number of positions: ＿＿
　　Direction:　Right＿＿　Left＿＿
Reflected?　Yes＿＿　　No＿＿
　　Axis:　V＿＿　H＿＿　D＿＿

B-112　

Rotated?　Yes＿＿　No＿＿
　　Number of positions: ＿＿
　　Direction:　Right＿＿　Left＿＿
Reflected?　Yes＿＿　　No＿＿
　　Axis:　V＿＿　H＿＿　D＿＿

SEQUENCES

PAPER FOLDING—SELECT

Match the folded sheet on the right with the corresponding unfolded sheet on the left. Write the correct letter on the line near each unfolded sheet.

B-113 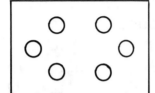 _____

a.

B-114 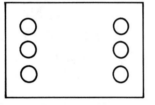 _____

b.

B-115 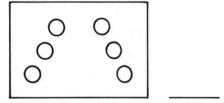 _____

c.

B-116 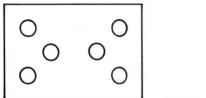 _____

d.

B-117 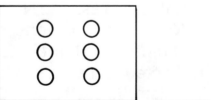 _____

e.

PAPER FOLDING—SELECT

Match the folded sheet on the right with the corresponding unfolded sheet on the left. Write the correct letter on the line near each unfolded sheet.

B-118　　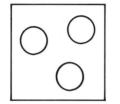　　　　　**a.**　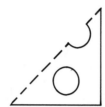

B-119　　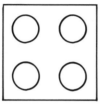　　　　　**b.**　

B-120　　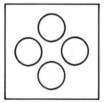　　　　　**c.**　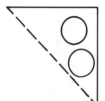

B-121　　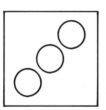　　　　　**d.**　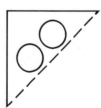

B-122　　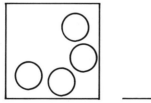　　　　　**e.**　

© 1985 MIDWEST PUBLICATIONS 93950

SEQUENCES

PAPER FOLDING—SELECT

Match the folded sheet on the right with the corresponding unfolded sheet on the left. Write the correct letter on the line near each unfolded sheet.

B-123 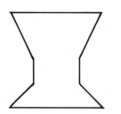 _____

a.

B-124  _____

b.

B-125 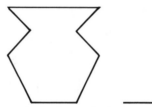 _____

c.

B-126 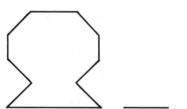 _____

d.

B-127 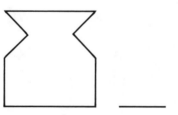 _____

e.

PAPER FOLDING—SELECT

Match the folded sheet on the right with the corresponding unfolded sheet on the left. Write the correct letter on the line near each unfolded sheet.

B-128  _____

a.

B-129 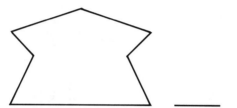 _____

b.

B-130 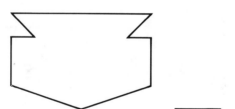 _____

c.

B-131  _____

d.

B-132 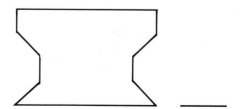 _____

e.

SEQUENCES

PAPER FOLDING—SELECT

Match the unfolded sheet on the right with the corresponding folded sheet on the left. Write the correct letter on the line near each folded sheet.

B-133
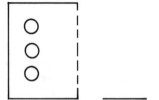

a.
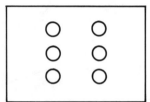

B-134
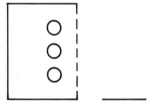

b.
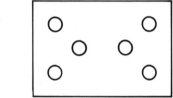

B-135
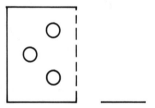

c.
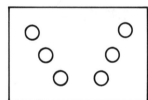

B-136
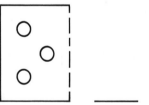

d.
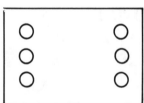

B-137
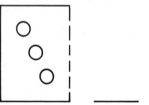

e.
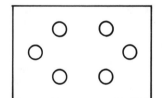

PAPER FOLDING—SELECT

Match the unfolded sheet on the right with the corresponding folded sheet on the left. Write the correct letter on the line near each folded sheet.

B-138
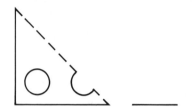

a.
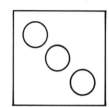

B-139

b.
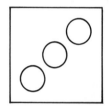

B-140
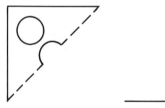

c.
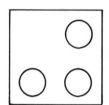

B-141
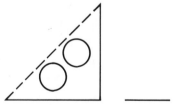

d.
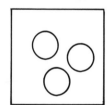

B-142
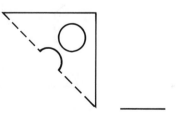

e.
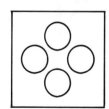

SEQUENCES

PAPER FOLDING—SELECT

Match the unfolded sheet on the right with the corresponding folded sheet on the left. Write the correct letter on the line near each folded sheet.

B-143    **a.**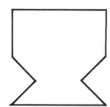

B-144 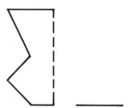   **b.**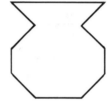

B-145 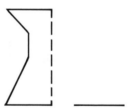   **c.**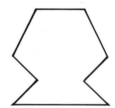

B-146 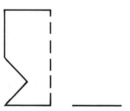   **d.**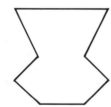

B-147 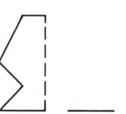   **e.**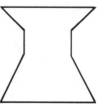

PAPER FOLDING—SELECT

Match the unfolded sheet on the right with the corresponding folded sheet on the left. Write the correct letter on the line near each folded sheet.

B-148
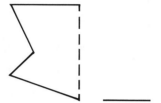

a.
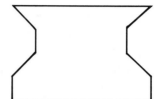

B-149
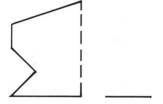

b.
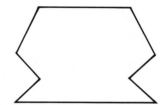

B-150

c.
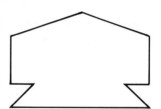

B-151
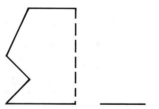

d.
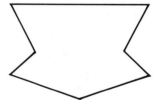

B-152
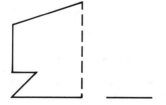

e.
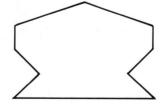

SEQUENCES

PAPER FOLDING—SUPPLY

Here are five sheets of paper that will be folded along the dotted line. Draw each as it will look when folded.

B-153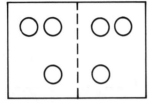

B-154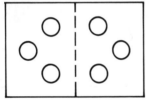

B-155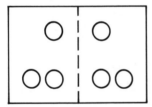

B-156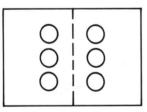

B-157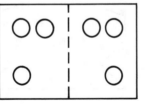

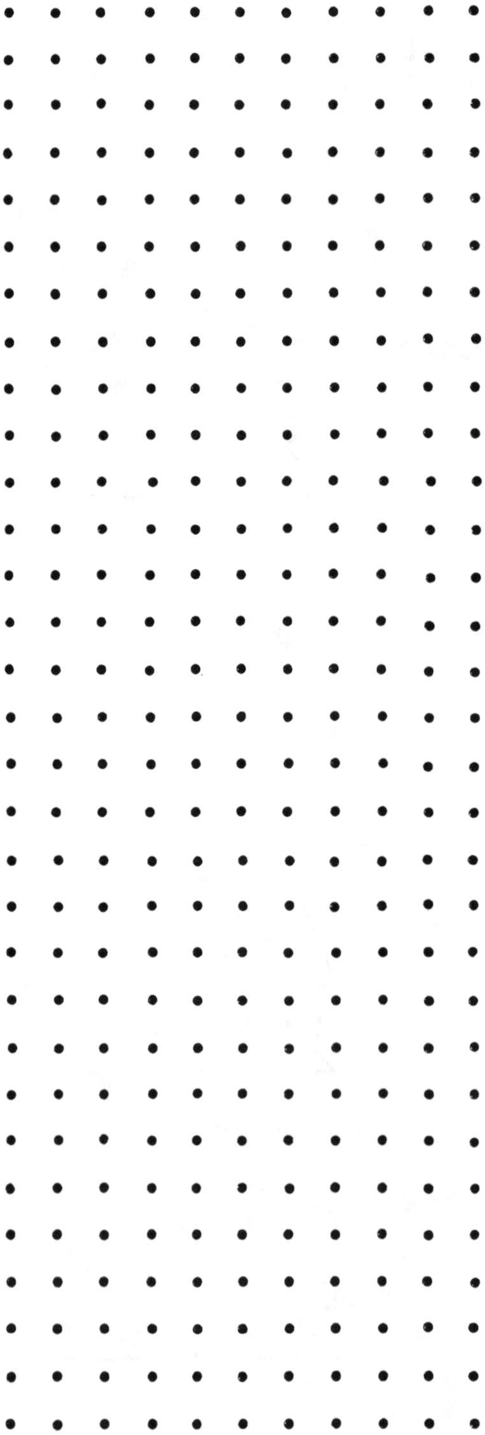

PAPER FOLDING—SUPPLY

Here are four sheets of paper that will be folded along the
dotted line. Draw each as it will look when folded.

B-158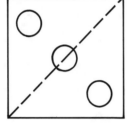

B-159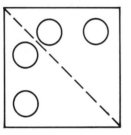

B-160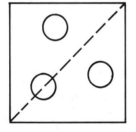

B-161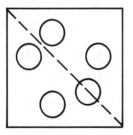

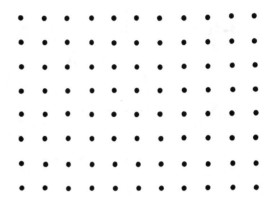
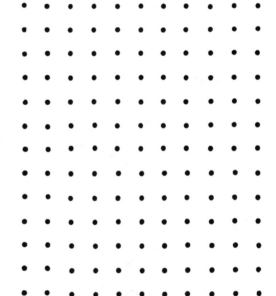
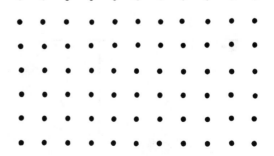

SEQUENCES

PAPER FOLDING—SUPPLY

Here are five sheets of paper that will be folded along the dotted line. Draw each as it will look when folded.

B-162
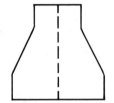

B-163
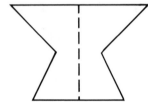

B-164
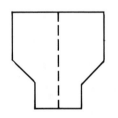

B-165
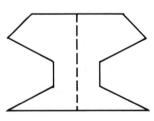

B-166
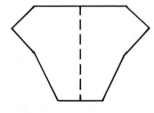

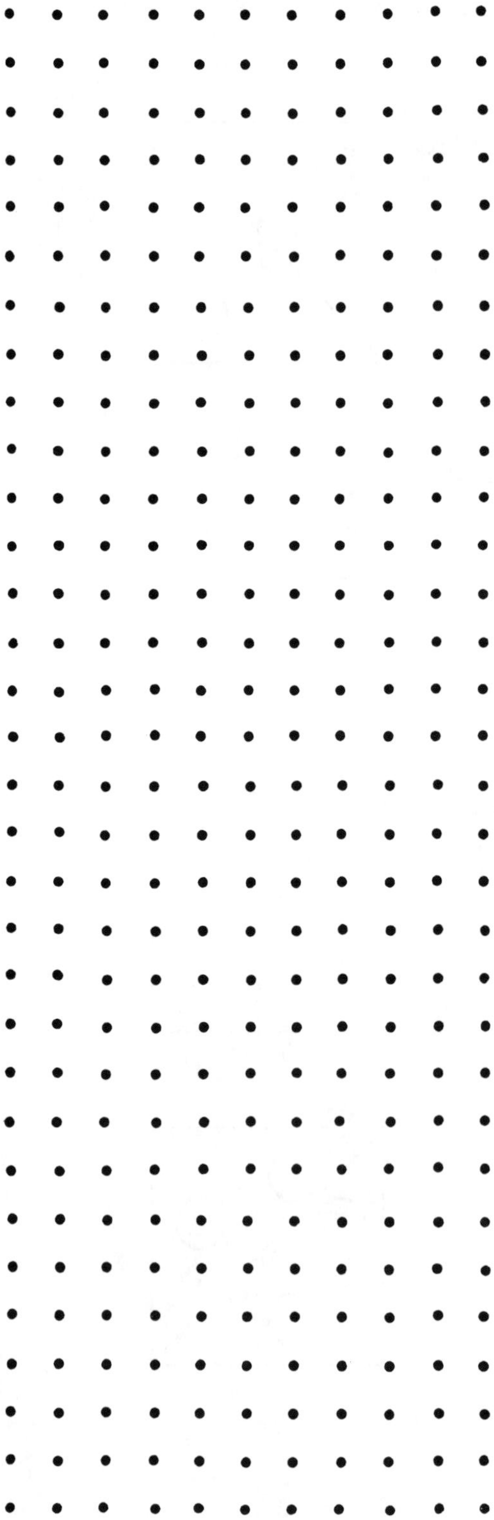

PAPER FOLDING—SUPPLY

Here are five sheets of paper that have been folded along the dotted line. Draw each as it will look when unfolded.

B-167

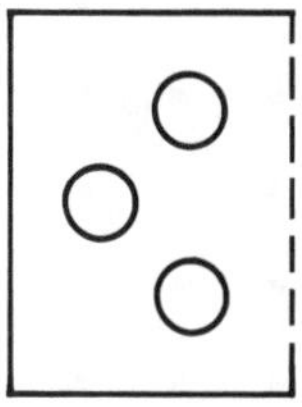

B-168

B-169

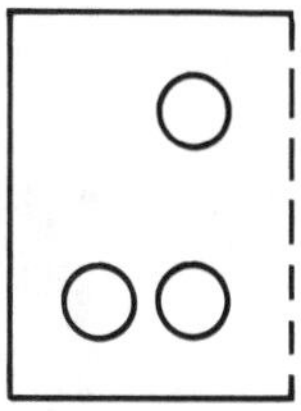

B-170

B-171

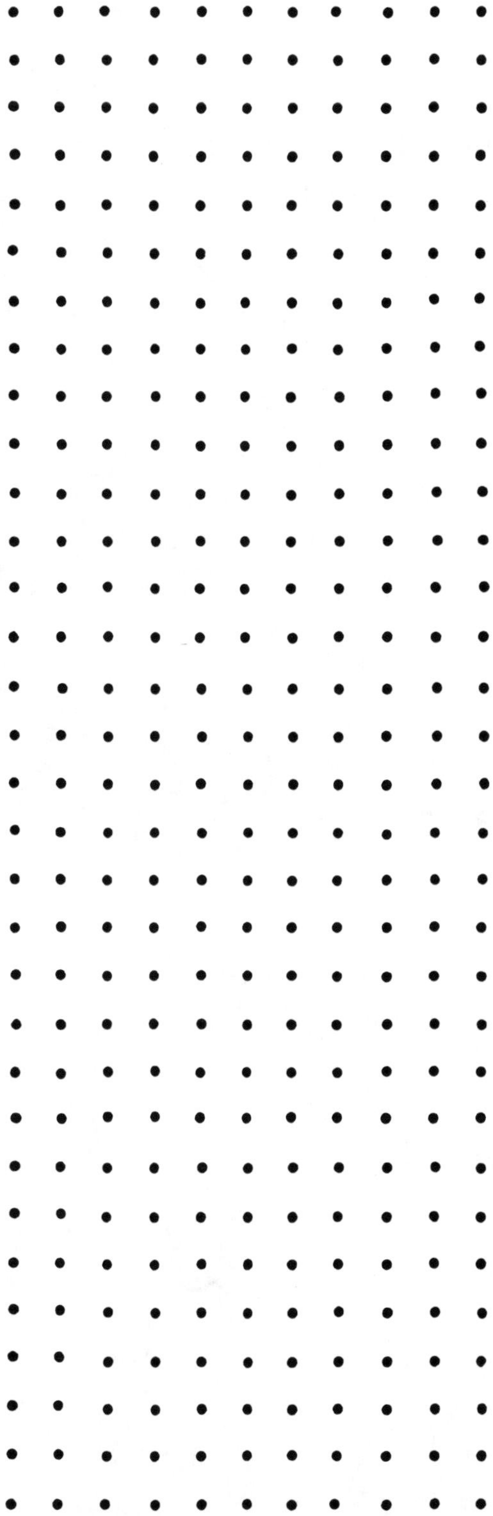

SEQUENCES

PAPER FOLDING—SUPPLY

Here are four sheets of paper that have been folded along the dotted line. Draw each as it will look when unfolded.

B-172

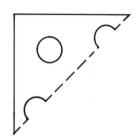

B-173

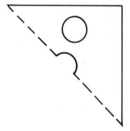

B-174

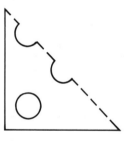

B-175

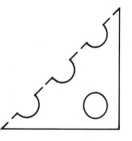

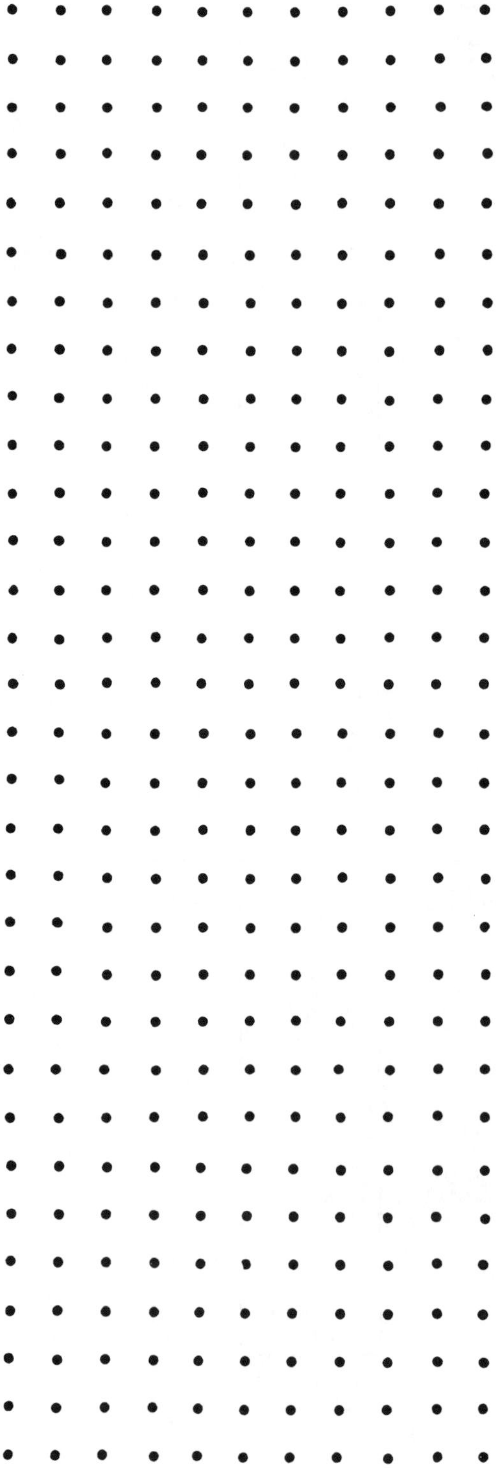

PAPER FOLDING—SUPPLY

Here are five sheets of paper that have been folded along the dotted line. Draw each as it will look when unfolded.

B-176
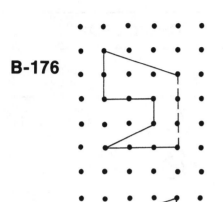
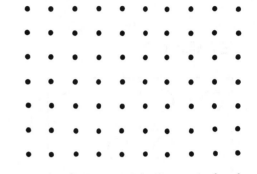

B-177
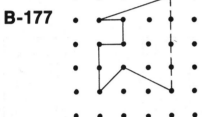
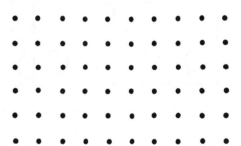

B-178
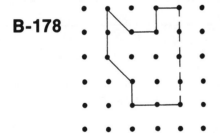

B-179
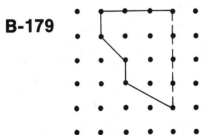
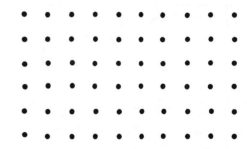

B-180
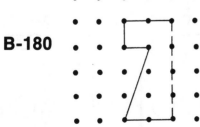

SEQUENCES

TWO-AXIS PAPER FOLDING—SELECT

Here are two sheets of paper with holes punched in them. The sheets are to be folded flat along the dotted lines. How will each sheet look after it has been folded twice? Circle the letter above the correct answer.

EXAMPLE:

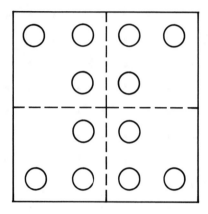

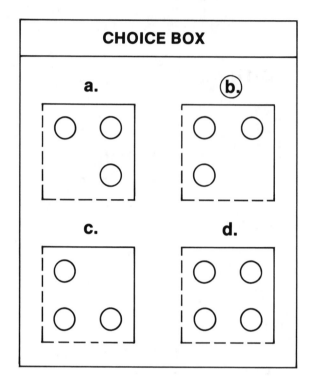

B-181

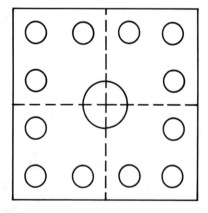

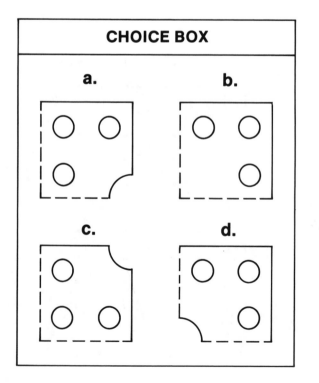

TWO-AXIS PAPER FOLDING—SELECT

Here are two sheets of paper with holes punched in them. The sheets are to be folded flat along the dotted lines. How will each sheet look after it has been folded twice? Circle the letter above the correct answer.

B-182

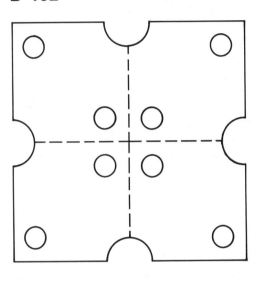

CHOICE BOX

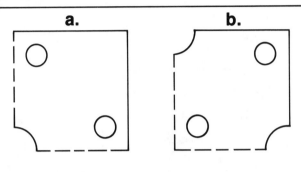

a.   b.

c.   d.

B-183

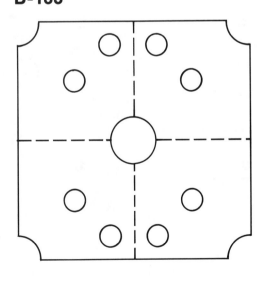

CHOICE BOX

a.   b.

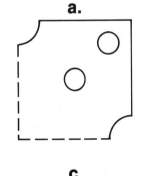 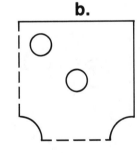

c.   d.

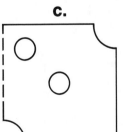 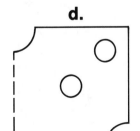

SEQUENCES

TWO-AXIS PAPER FOLDING—SELECT

Here are two sheets of paper with holes punched in them. The sheets are to be folded flat along the dotted lines. How will each sheet look after it has been folded twice? Circle the letter above the correct answer.

B-184

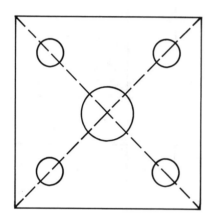

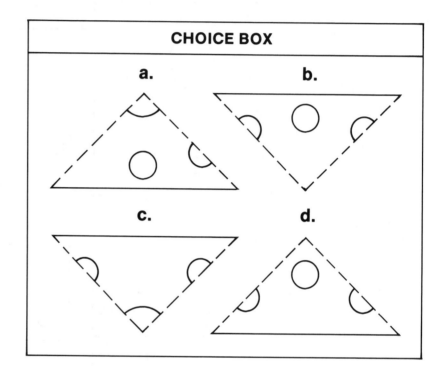

B-185

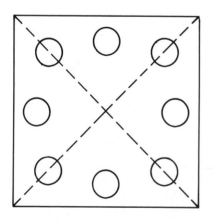

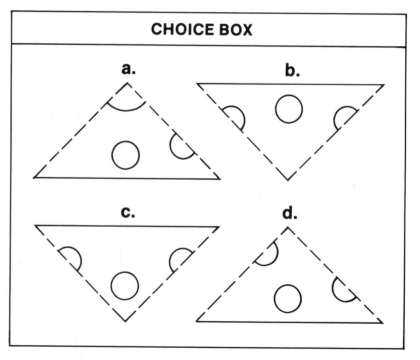

TWO-AXIS PAPER FOLDING—SELECT

Here are two sheets of paper that will be folded along the dotted lines. How will each sheet look after it has been folded twice? Circle the letter above the correct answer.

B-186

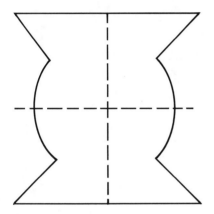

CHOICE BOX

a. 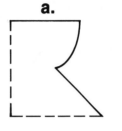　**b.**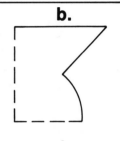

c. 　**d.**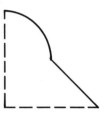

B-187

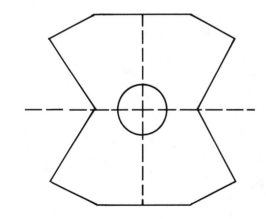

CHOICE BOX

a. 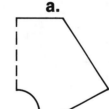　**b.**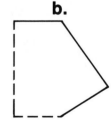

c. 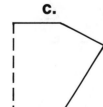　**d.**

SEQUENCES

TWO-AXIS PAPER FOLDING—SELECT

Match each twice-folded sheet on the right with the corresponding sheet on the left. Write the correct answer on the line near each unfolded sheet.

B-188

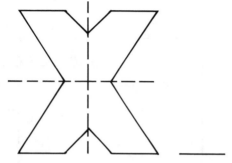

a.

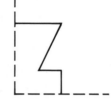

B-189

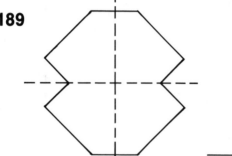

b.

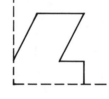

c.

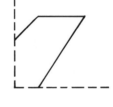

B-190

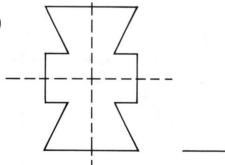

d.

B-191

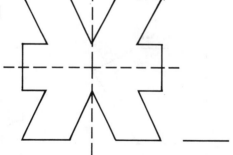

e.

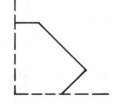

TWO-AXIS PAPER FOLDING—SELECT

Match each twice-folded sheet on the right with the corresponding unfolded sheet on the left. Write the correct letter on the line near each unfolded sheet.

B-192

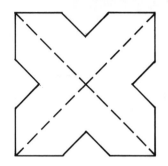

_____

a.

B-193

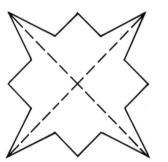

_____

b.

B-194

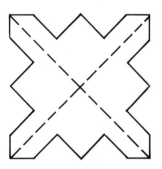

_____

c.

B-195

_____

d.

TWO-AXIS PAPER FOLDING—SELECT

Match each unfolded sheet on the right with the corresponding twice-folded sheet on the left. Write the correct answer on the line near each folded sheet.

B-196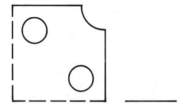

a.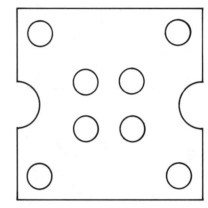

B-197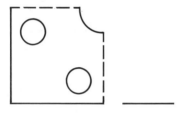

b.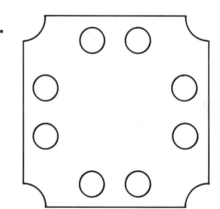

B-198

c.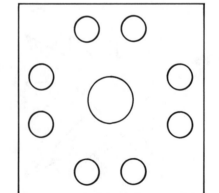

B-199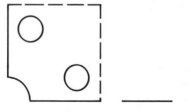

TWO-AXIS PAPER FOLDING—SELECT

Match each unfolded sheet on the right with the corresponding twice-folded sheet on the left. Write the correct answer on the line near each folded sheet.

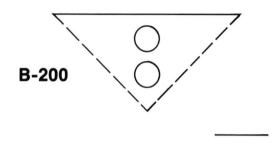

B-200 _____

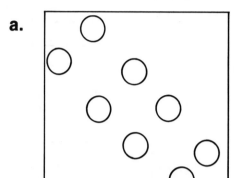

a.

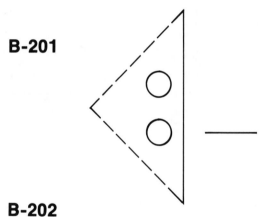

B-201 _____

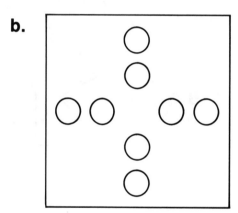

b.

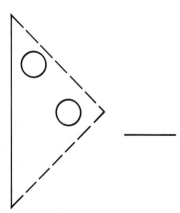

B-202 _____

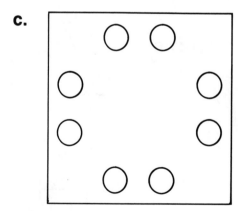

c.

SEQUENCES

TWO-AXIS PAPER FOLDING—SELECT

Match each unfolded sheet on the right with the corresponding twice-folded sheet on the left. Write the correct answer on the line near each folded sheet.

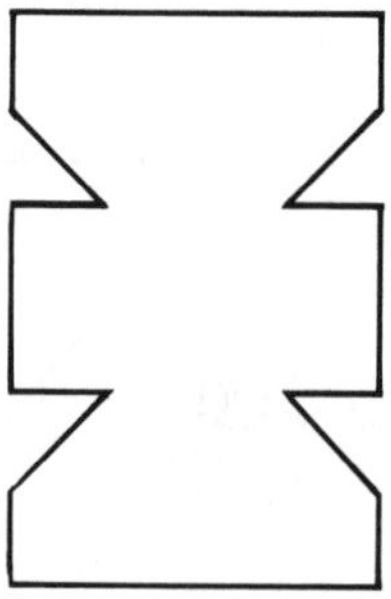

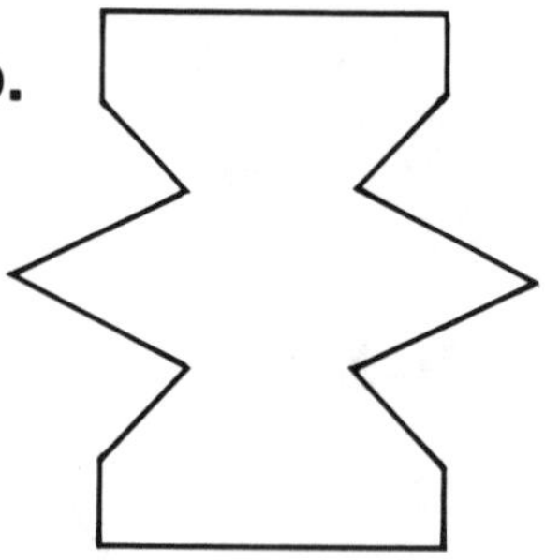

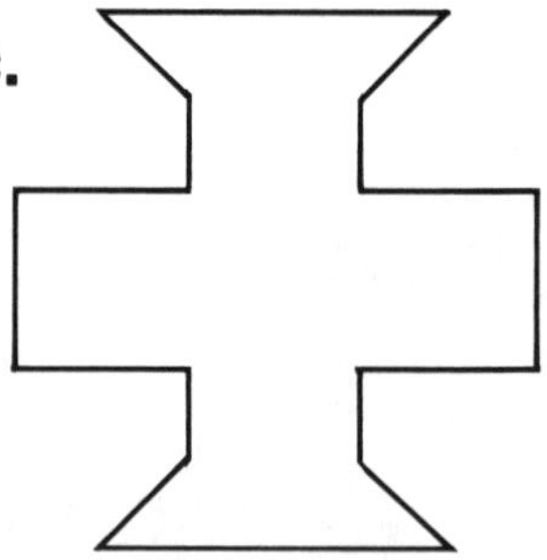

B-203

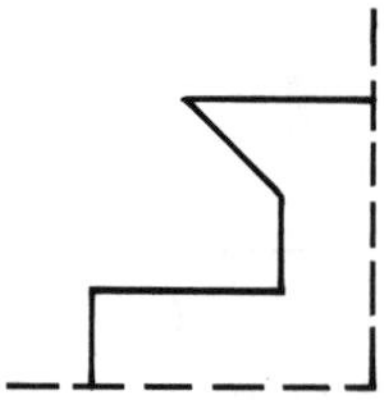

a.

B-204

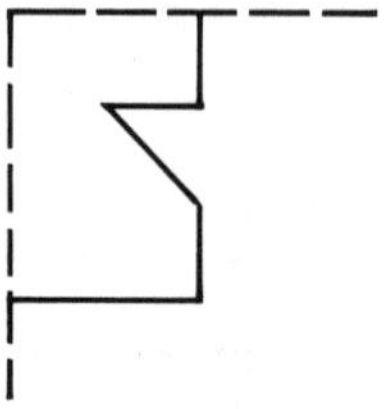

b.

B-205

c.

B-206

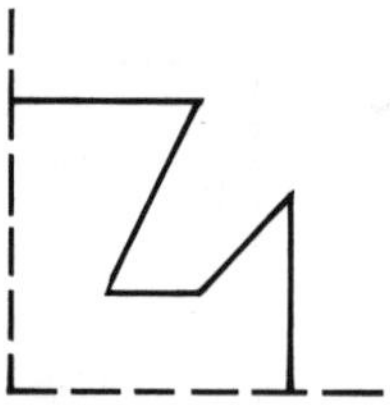

d.

B-207

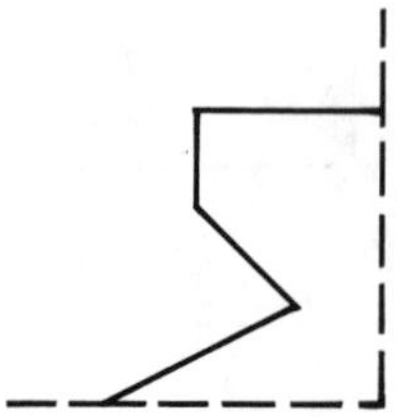

TWO-AXIS PAPER FOLDING—SELECT

Match each unfolded sheet on the right with the corresponding twice-folded sheet on the left. Write the correct answer on the line near each folded sheet.

a.

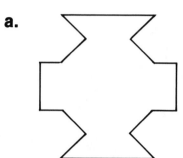

B-208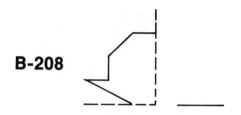

b.

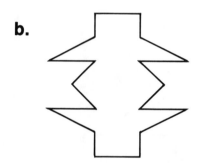

B-209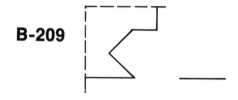

B-210

c.

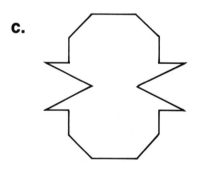

B-211

d.

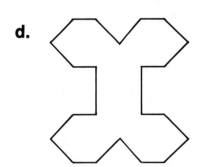

B-212

SEQUENCES

TWO-AXIS PAPER FOLDING—SELECT

Match each unfolded sheet on the right with the corresponding twice-folded sheet on the left. Write the correct answer on the line near each folded sheet.

B-213

a.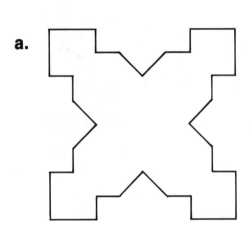

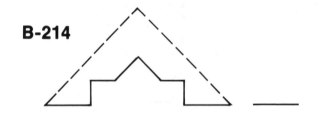

B-214

b.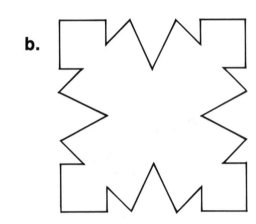

B-215

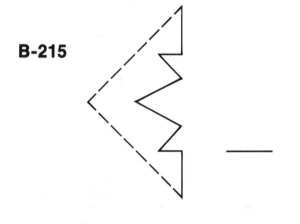

c.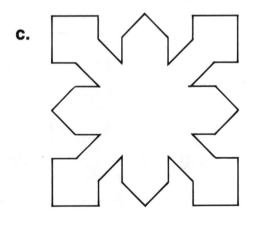

B-216

TWO-AXIS PAPER FOLDING—SUPPLY

The sheets of paper below are to be folded twice along the dotted lines. Draw the four possible folded views for each sheet on the dot grid.

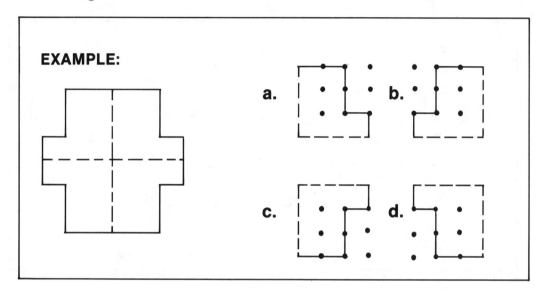

EXAMPLE:

a.　b.

c.　d.

SEQUENCES

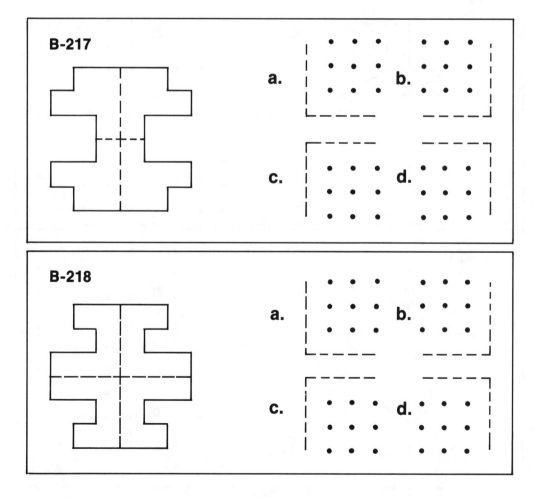

B-217

a.　b.

c.　d.

B-218

a.　b.

c.　d.

TWO-AXIS PAPER FOLDING—SUPPLY

The sheets of paper below are to be folded twice along the dotted lines. Draw the four possible folded views for each sheet on the dot grid.

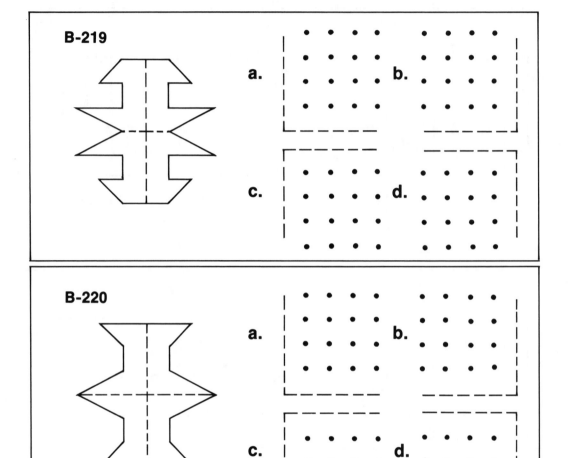

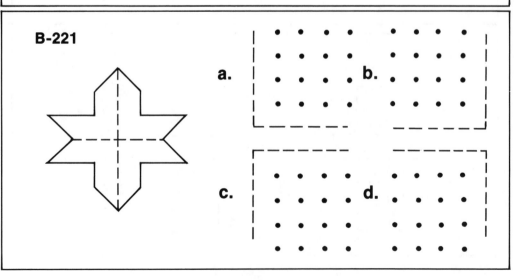

TWO-AXIS PAPER FOLDING—SUPPLY

The sheets of paper below are to be folded twice along the dotted lines. Draw each sheet as it will look when folded. Draw only one view.

B-222

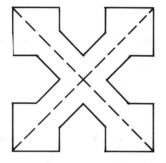

B-223

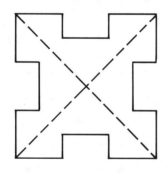

B-224

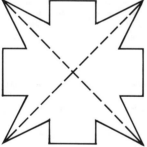

B-225

SEQUENCES

TWO-AXIS PAPER FOLDING—SUPPLY

The sheets of paper below are to be folded twice along the dotted lines. Draw each sheet as it will look when folded. Draw only one view.

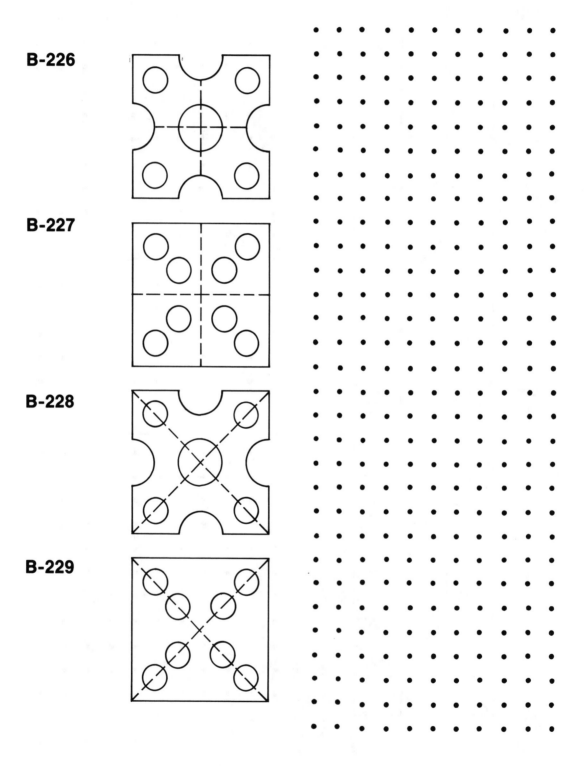

B-226

B-227

B-228

B-229

© 1985 MIDWEST PUBLICATIONS 93950

TWO-AXIS PAPER FOLDING—SUPPLY

Here are four sheets of paper that have been folded twice along the dotted lines. Draw each sheet as it will look when unfolded.

B-230
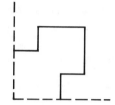

B-231
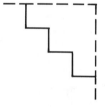

B-232
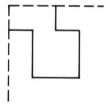

B-233
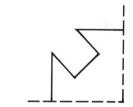

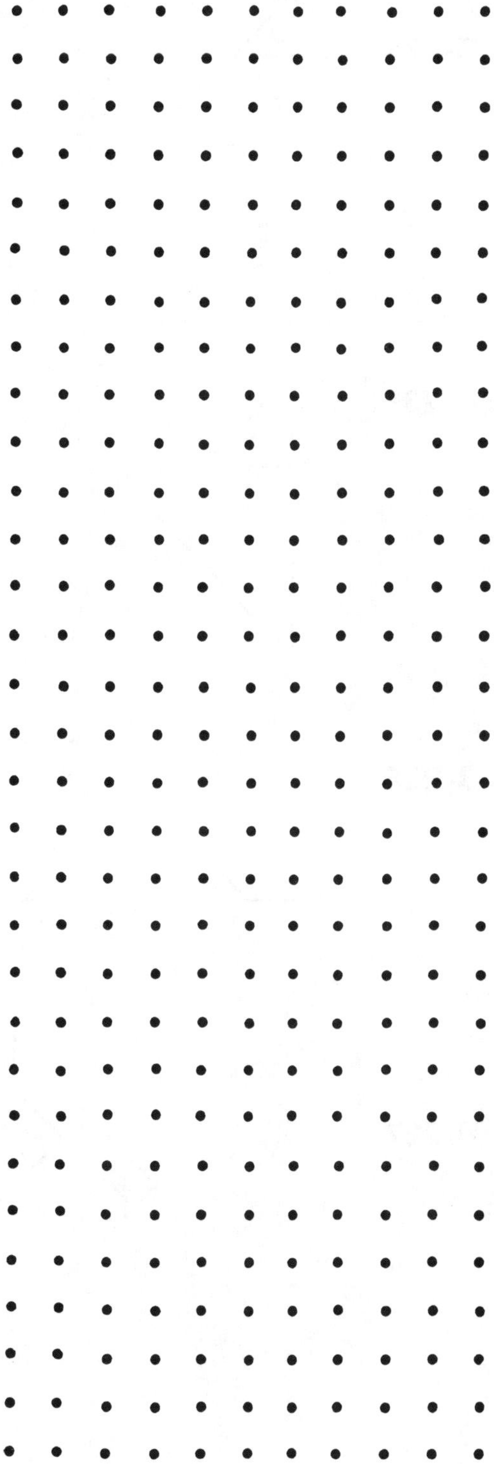

SEQUENCES

TWO-AXIS PAPER FOLDING—SUPPLY

Here are four sheets of paper that have been folded twice along the dotted lines. Draw each sheet as it will look when unfolded.

B-234

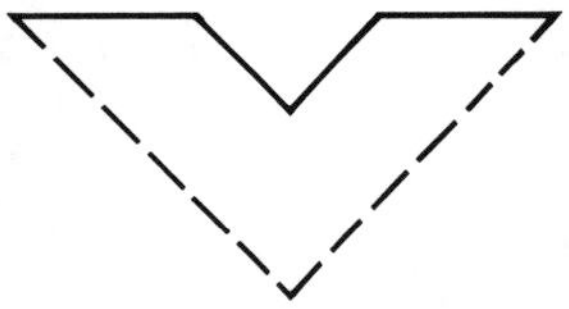

B-235

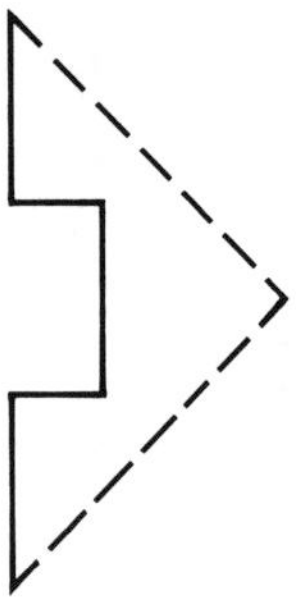

B-236

B-237

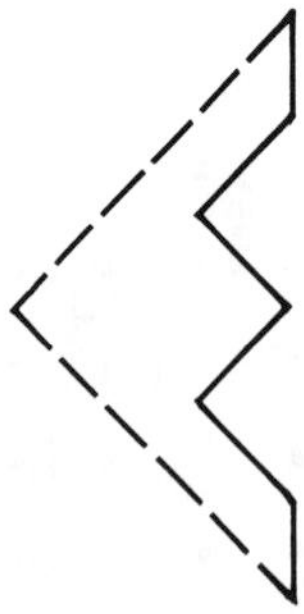

TWO-AXIS PAPER FOLDING—SUPPLY

Here are four sheets of paper that have been folded twice along the dotted lines. Draw each sheet as it will look when unfolded.

B-238

B-239

B-240

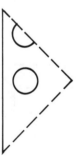

B-241

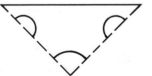

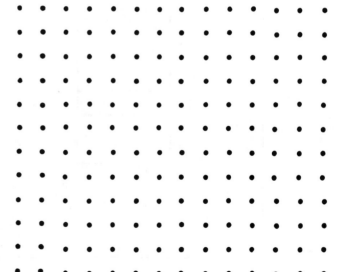

PATTERN FOLDING—SELECT

Each pattern on the left is a wrapper for one of the solids on the right. Draw a circle around the correct solid.

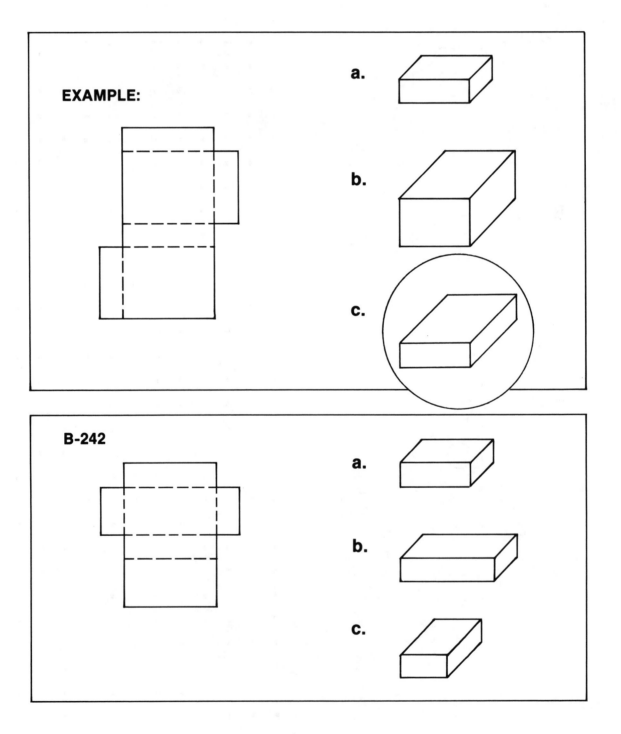

© 1985 MIDWEST PUBLICATIONS 93950

PATTERN FOLDING—SELECT

Each pattern on the left is a wrapper for one of the solids on the right. Draw a circle around the correct solid.

B-243

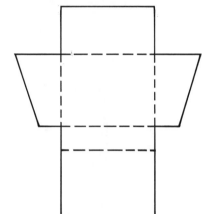

a.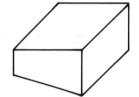

b.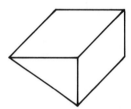

c.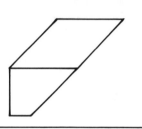

B-244

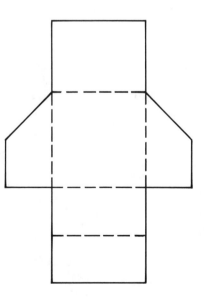

a.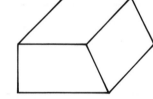

b.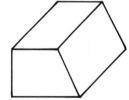

c.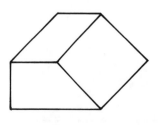

PATTERN FOLDING—SELECT

Each pattern on the left is a wrapper for one of the solids on
the right. Draw a circle around the correct solid.

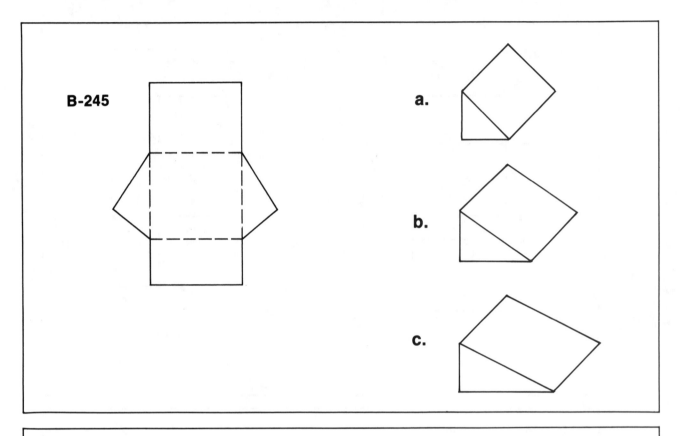

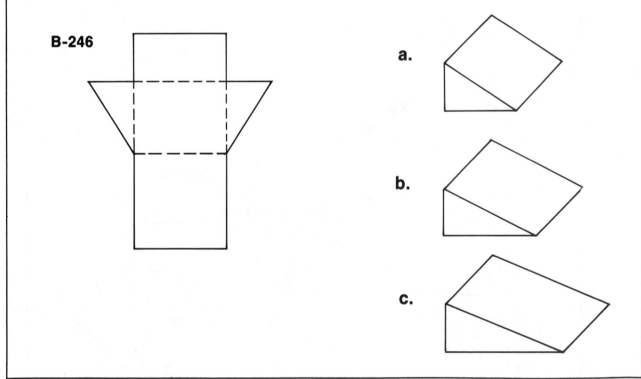

PATTERN FOLDING—SELECT

Each pattern on the left is a wrapper for one of the solids on the right. Draw a circle around the correct solid.

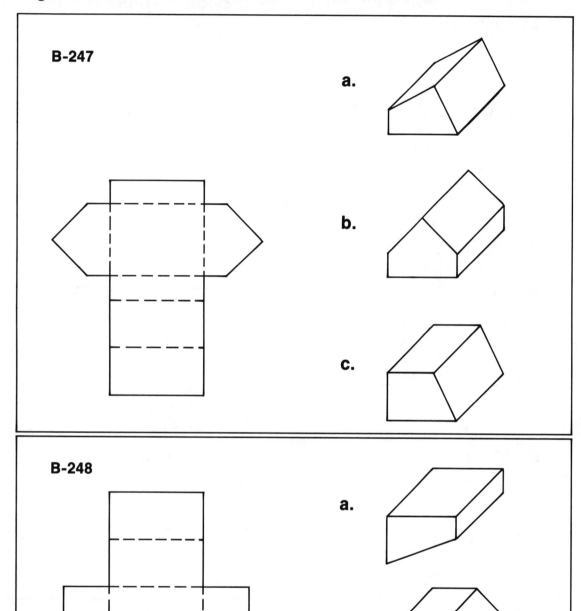

B-247

a.

b.

c.

B-248

a.

b.

c.

SEQUENCES

PATTERN FOLDING—MATCHING

Each solid on the left can be covered by one of the wrappers on the right. Write the letter of the matching wrapper on the line by each solid.

a.

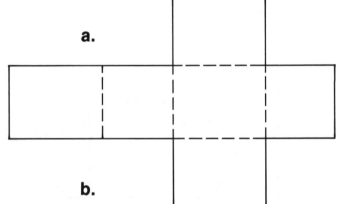

EXAMPLE:

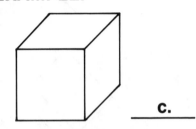

c. _____

b.

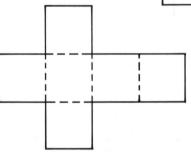

B-249

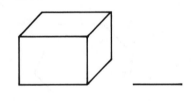

_____

B-250

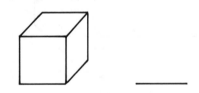

_____

c.

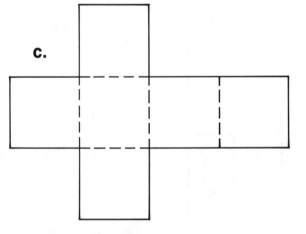

B-251

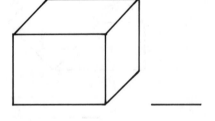

_____ **d.**

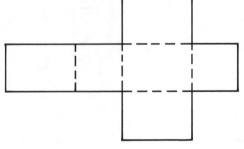

PATTERN FOLDING—MATCHING

Each solid on the left can be covered by one of the wrappers on the right. Write the letter of the matching wrapper on the line by each solid.

a.

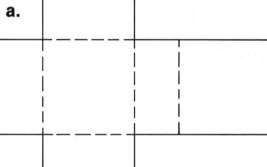

B-252

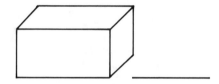

_____

b.

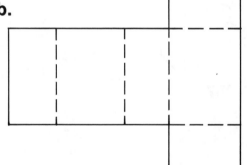

B-253

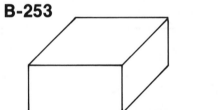

_____

c.

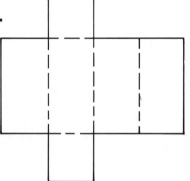

B-254

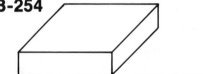

_____

B-255

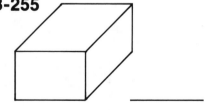

_____

d.

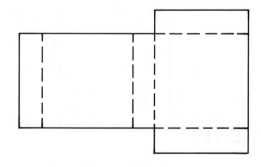

SEQUENCES

PATTERN FOLDING—MATCHING

Each solid on the left can be covered by one of the wrappers on the right. Write the letter of the matching wrapper on the line by each solid.

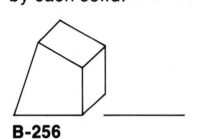

B-256 _____

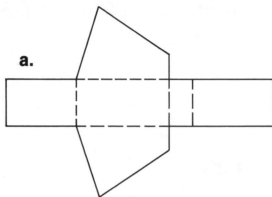

a.

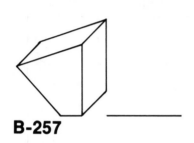

B-257 _____

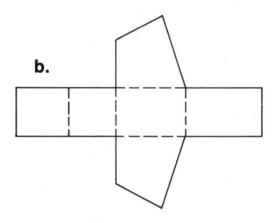

b.

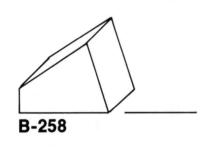

B-258 _____

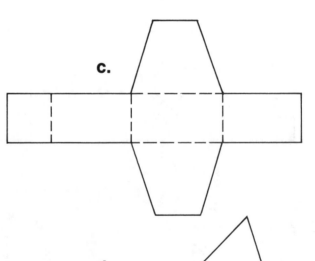

c.

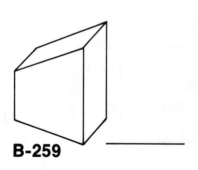

B-259 _____

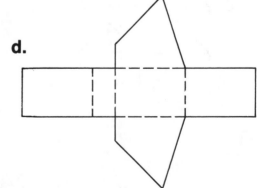

d.

SELECTING PATTERN PIECES

In the next exercises it is necessary to identify the size of solids. When drawing solids, it is difficult to represent the appearance of "depth." Here are the rules that were followed in drawing the solids.

Here is a picture of a cube which has sides that are four units long (1 inch).

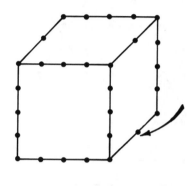

This line visually represents a side four units long. Note that, in order to show depth, this side is drawn as the diagonal of a square having sides two units long.

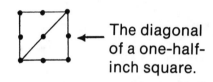

The diagonal of a one-half-inch square.

Look what happens if the depth is drawn in a true inch (four units).

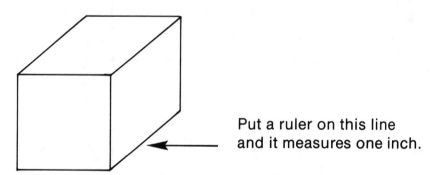

Put a ruler on this line and it measures one inch.

With a true inch in depth the solid no longer looks like a cube. There are many ways to give the illusion of depth. A very simple way is to make the depth line the diagonal of a square (a line from corner to corner).

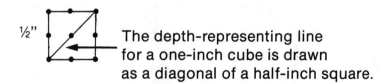

½"

The depth-representing line for a one-inch cube is drawn as a diagonal of a half-inch square.

SEQUENCES

SELECTING PATTERN PIECES

Examine the solid on the left. Decide which of the shapes in the box can be used as a pattern for each of the sides of the solid. Cross out the unused shapes. Mark the pattern pieces used with the number needed.

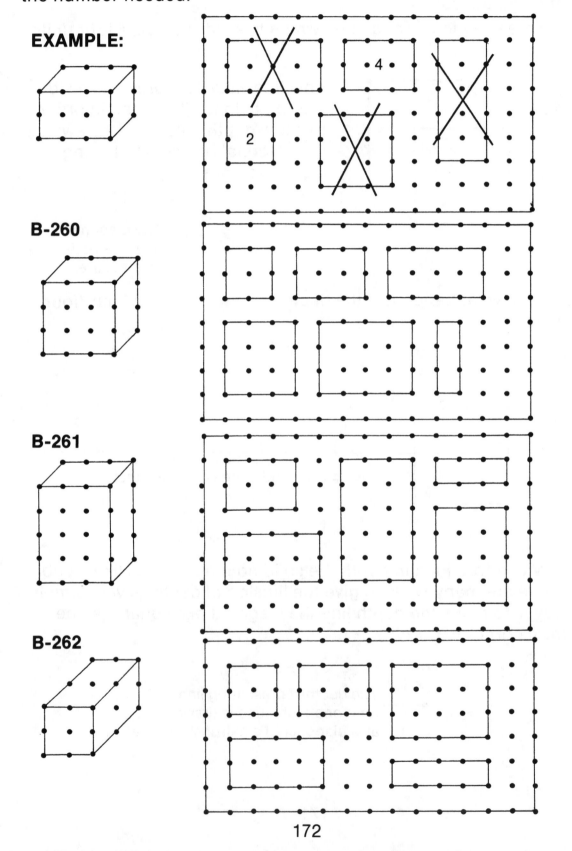

EXAMPLE:

B-260

B-261

B-262

© 1985 MIDWEST PUBLICATIONS 93950

SELECTING PATTERN PIECES

Examine the solid on the left. Decide which of the shapes in the box can be used as a pattern for each of the sides of the solid. Cross out the unused shapes. Mark the pattern pieces used with the number needed.

B-263
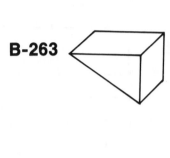
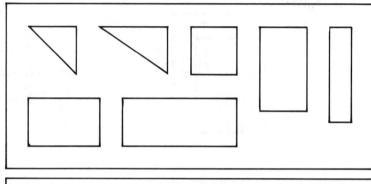

B-264
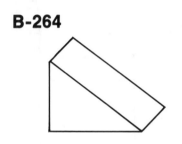
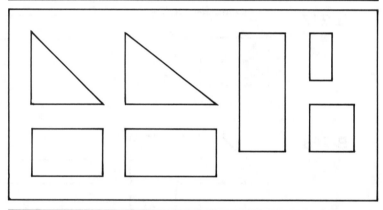

B-265
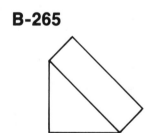
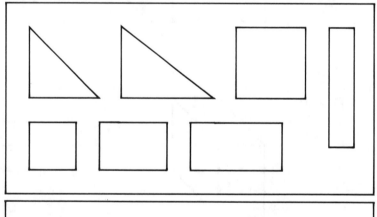

B-266
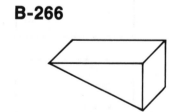
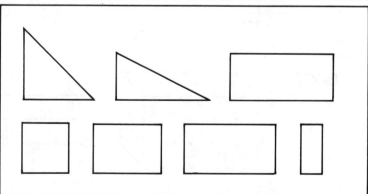

MATCHING PATTERN PIECES

Examine each solid on the left. Decide which shape on the right can be used as a pattern for each side of the solid. Decide how many of each are needed.

a.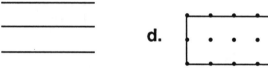

EXAMPLE:

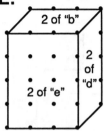

$$\frac{b = 2}{\frac{d = 2}{e = 2}}$$

b.

B-267

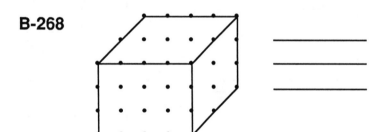

c.

d.

B-268

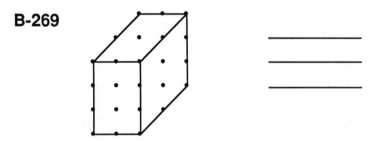

e.

f.

B-269

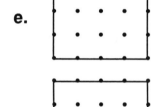

g.

h.

B-270

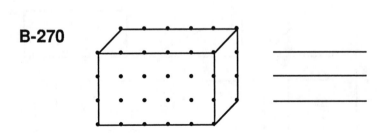

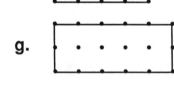

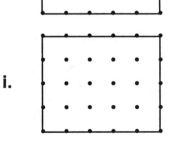

i.

MATCHING PATTERN PIECES

Examine each solid on the left. Decide which shape on the right can be used as a pattern for each side of the solid. Decide how many of each are needed.

SEQUENCES

a.

b.

B-271

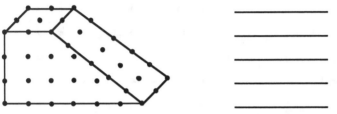

c.

d.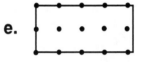

e.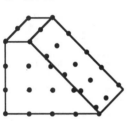

B-272

f.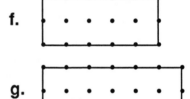

g.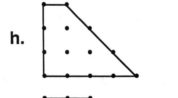

h.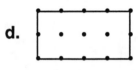

B-273

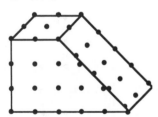

i.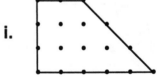

j.

B-274

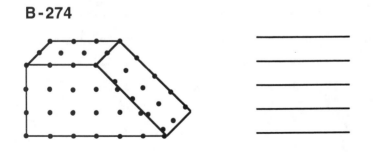

k.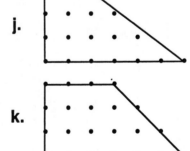

PRODUCE A PATTERN

Draw a wrapper pattern for the solids on the left. Use the dot grid as a guide. The **top** view has been given.

B-275

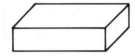

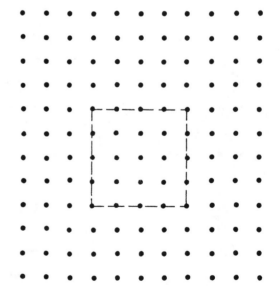

B-276

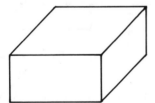

PRODUCE A PATTERN

Draw a wrapper pattern for the solids on the left. Use the dot grid as a guide. The **bottom** view has been given.

B-277

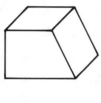

B-278

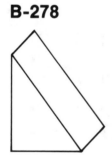

B-279

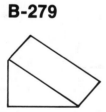

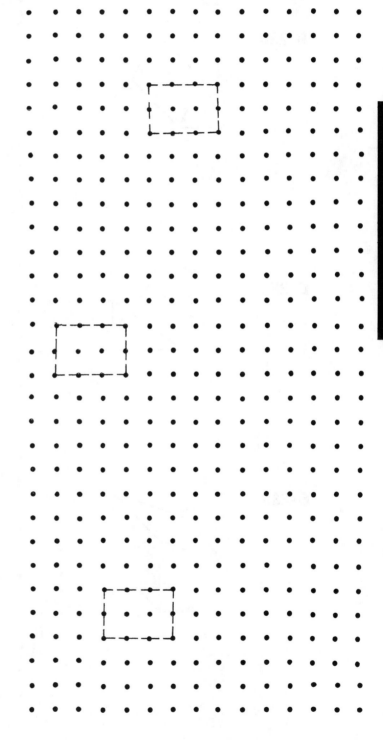

PRODUCE A PATTERN

Draw a wrapper pattern for the solids on the left. Use the dot grid as a guide. The **bottom** view has been given.

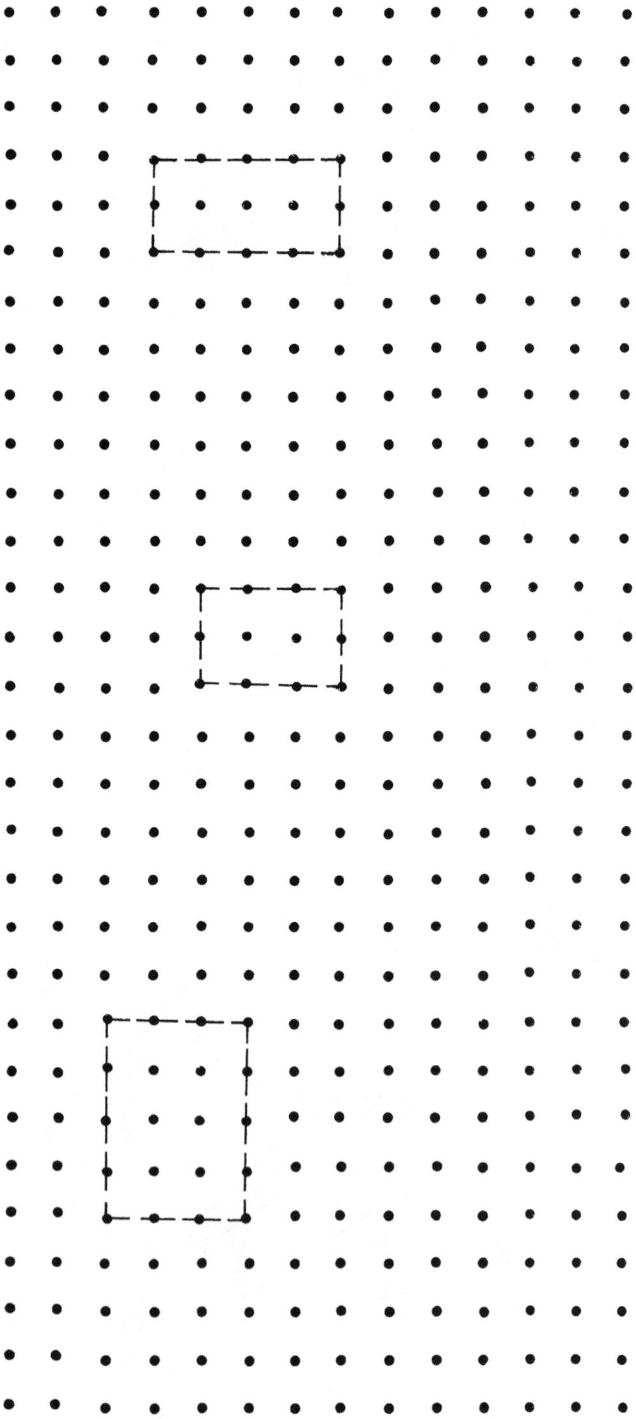

B-280

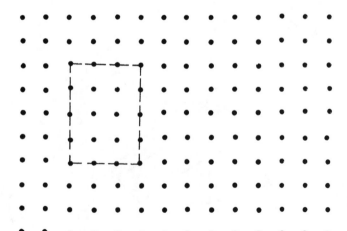

B-281

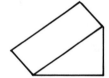

B-282

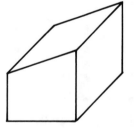

FOLDING CUBE PATTERNS—SELECT

Some of these patterns, when folded, will make a cube. Some will not. Mentally fold each pattern and mark it **Y** if it will make a cube, or **N** if it will not.

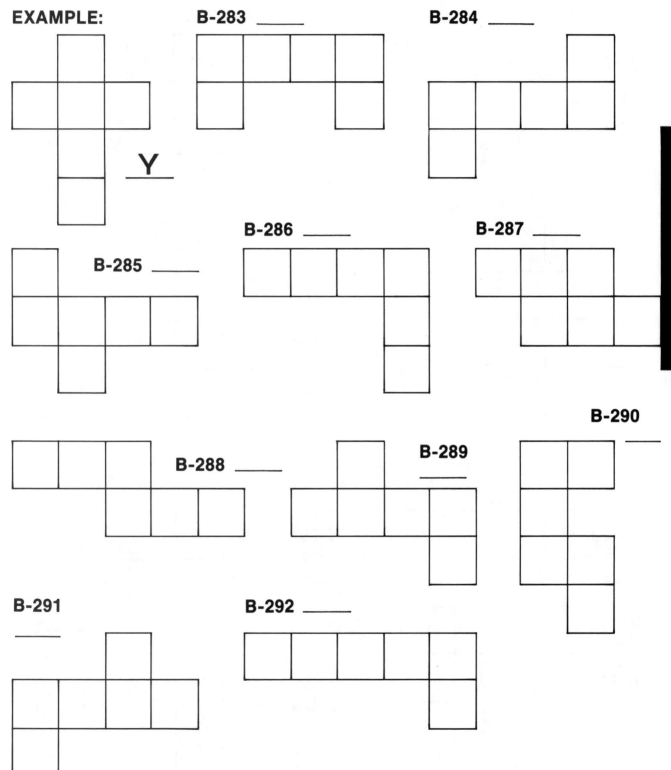

EXAMPLE: Y

B-283 _____

B-284 _____

B-285 _____

B-286 _____

B-287 _____

B-288 _____

B-289 _____

B-290 _____

B-291 _____

B-292 _____

© 1985 MIDWEST PUBLICATIONS 93950

SEQUENCES

FOLDING CUBE PATTERNS—SELECT

Examine the cube. Mentally fold each pattern. Are the locations and markings on the pattern correct to form the given cube? Mark each pattern **Y** if it will form the given cube, or **N** if it will not.

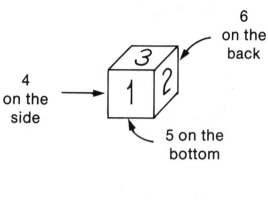

4 on the side

6 on the back

3

5 on the bottom

EXAMPLE:

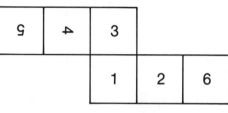

Y

B-293

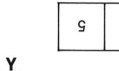

____

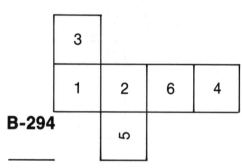

B-294

____

B-295

____

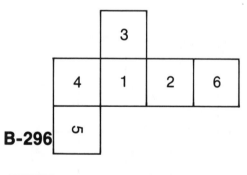

B-296

____

B-297

____

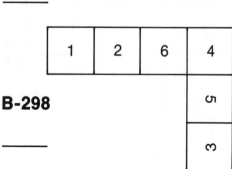

B-298

____

B-299

____

© 1985 MIDWEST PUBLICATIONS 93950

FOLDING CUBE PATTERNS—SUPPLY

Examine the cube. Mentally fold each pattern. Mark each face of the pattern with the correct number to make the given cube.

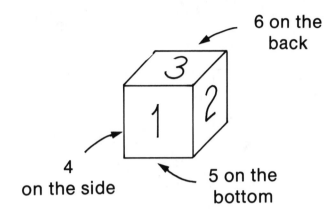

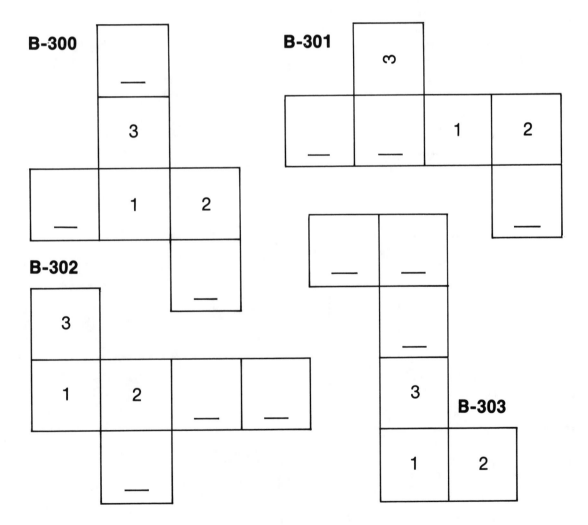

© 1985 MIDWEST PUBLICATIONS 93950

SEQUENCES

FOLDING CUBE PATTERNS—SUPPLY

Examine the cube. Mentally fold each pattern. Mark each face
of the pattern with the correct number to make the given cube.

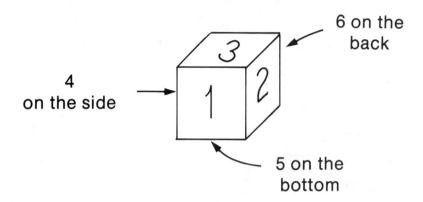

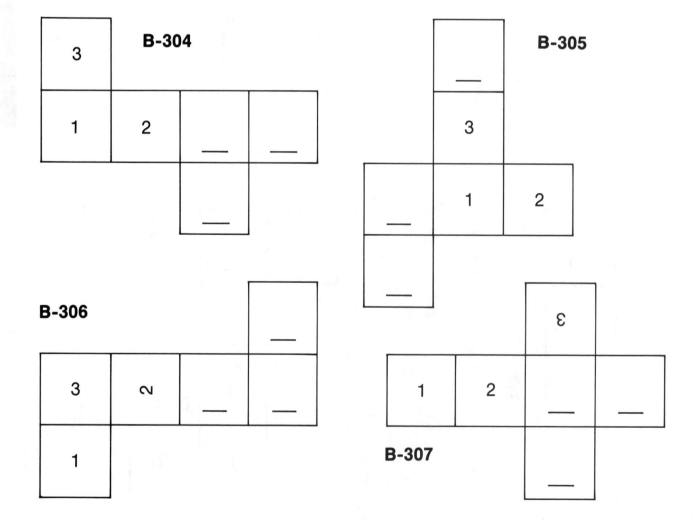

ROTATING CUBES

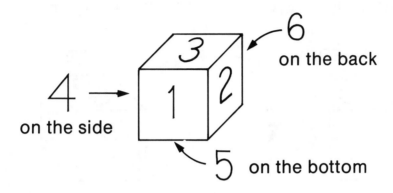

ROTATIONS — ABOUT AN UP-DOWN LINE

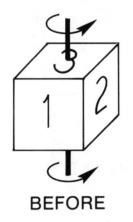

BEFORE   **AFTER ROTATION**

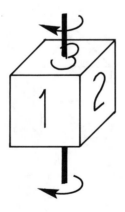

This second rotation is in a direction opposite to the first rotation.

© 1985 MIDWEST PUBLICATIONS 93950

ROTATING CUBES

ROTATIONS — ABOUT A LEFT-RIGHT LINE

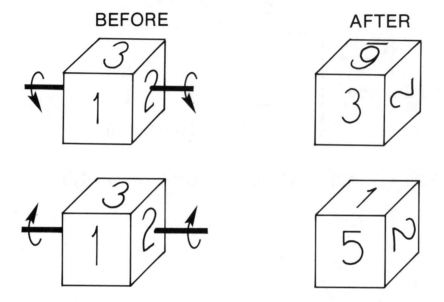

BEFORE　　　　　　　　　　　　　AFTER

ROTATIONS — ABOUT A LINE IN AND OUT OF THE FRONT FACE

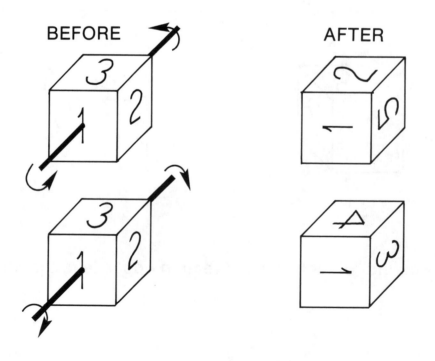

BEFORE　　　　　　　　　　　　　AFTER

© 1985 MIDWEST PUBLICATIONS 93950

ROTATING CUBES—SELECT

Examine the changes in position of the first three cubes. Decide how the cube is rotating. Select the cube from the choice box that shows the next position in the sequence. Circle the letter of the correct cube.

EXAMPLE:

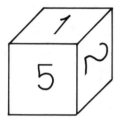 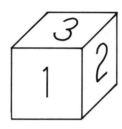 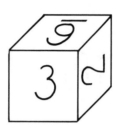

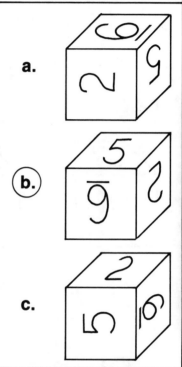

CHOICE BOX

a.

b.

c.

SEQUENCES

B-308

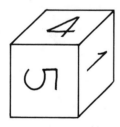 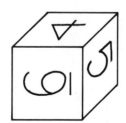 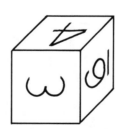

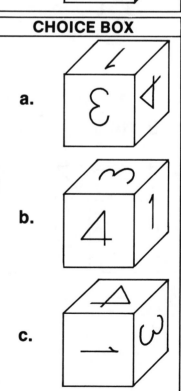

CHOICE BOX

a.

b.

c.

ROTATING CUBES—SELECT

Examine the changes in position of the first three cubes.
Decide how the cube is rotating. Select the cube from the choice
box that shows the next position in the sequence. Circle the letter
of the correct cube.

B-309

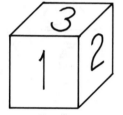  

B-310

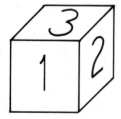 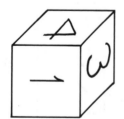 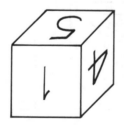

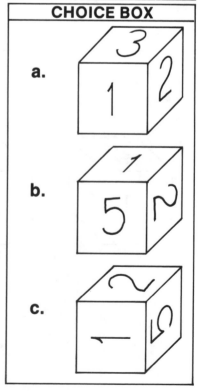

CHOICE BOX

a.

b.

c.

CHOICE BOX

a.

b.

c.

BUILDING THINKING SKILLS — BOOK 3

ROTATING CUBES—DESCRIBE

In each group of cubes, cube B and C represent rotations of cube A. Name the face described in each question.

SEQUENCES

EXAMPLE:

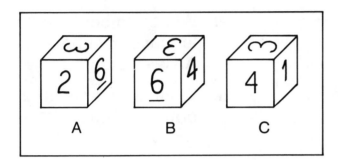

A   B   C

a. What number is on the back of cube A?
Answer __4__

b. What number is on the left face of cube C?
Answer __6__

c. What number is on the back of cube B?
Answer __1__

B-311

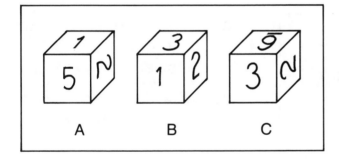

A   B   C

a. What number is on the back of cube A?
Answer _____

b. What number is on the bottom of cube C?
Answer _____

c. What number is on the back of cube C?
Answer _____

B-312

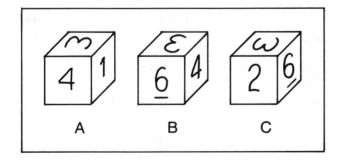

A   B   C

a. What number is on the left face of cube A?
Answer _____

b. What number is on the back of cube B?
Answer _____

c. What number is on the left face of cube B?
Answer _____

ROTATING CUBES—DESCRIBE

In each group of figures, cubes B and C represent rotations of cube A. Name the face described in each question.

B-313

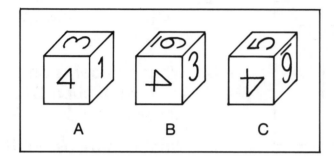

a. What number is on the left face of cube A?
Answer _____

b. What number is on the bottom of cube B?
Answer _____

c. What number is on the left face of cube C?
Answer _____

B-314

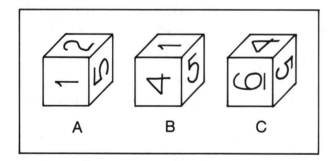

a. What number is on the bottom of cube B ?
Answer _____

b. What number is on the back of cube A?
Answer _____

c. What number is on the bottom of cube A?
Answer _____

B-315

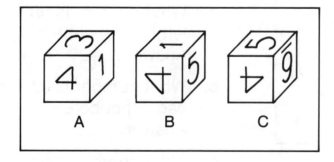

a. What number is on the left face of cube C?
Answer _____

b. What number is on the bottom of cube A?
Answer _____

c. What number is on the left face of cube A?
Answer _____

ROTATING CUBES—SUPPLY

Examine the changes in position of the first three cubes. Decide how the cube is rotating. Mark the last cube as it should look to continue the rotation sequence.

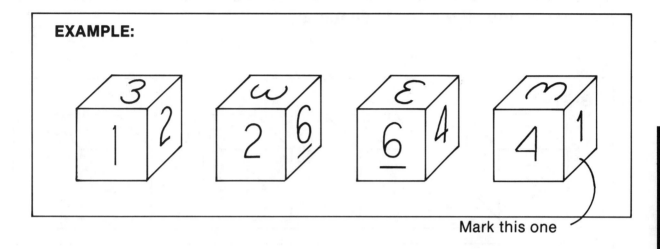

EXAMPLE:

Mark this one

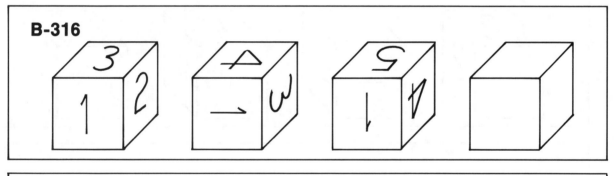

B-316

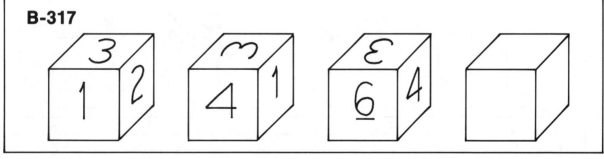

B-317

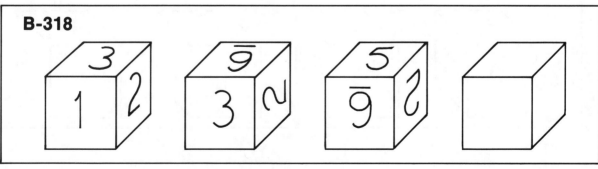

B-318

SEQUENCES

ROTATING CUBES—SUPPLY

Examine the changes in position of the first three cubes.
Decide how the cube is rotating. Mark the last cube as it should
look to continue the rotation sequence.

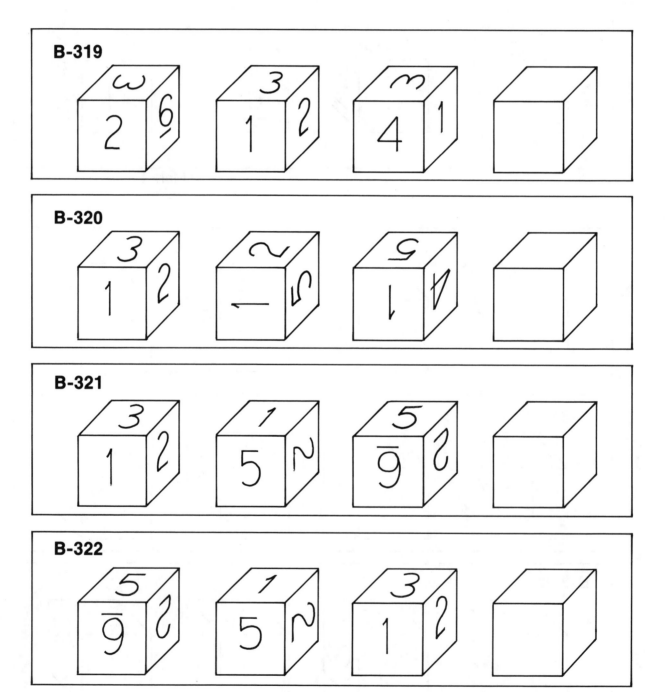

© 1985 MIDWEST PUBLICATIONS 93950

DESCRIBING CLASSES

Circle the letter in front of each statement that is true.

EXAMPLE:

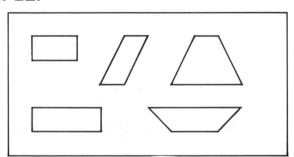

All the figures:

a. are rectangles
b. are white
c. are the same size
d. have four sides

"a" should not be circled; there are only two rectangles in the group.

"b" is true; all the figures **are** white.

"c" should not be circled; some of the figures are large and others small.

"d" is true; all the figures **do** have four sides.

C-1

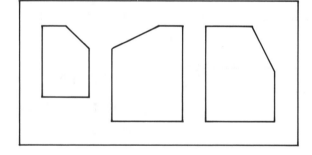

Each figure has:

a. three square corners
b. four sides
c. five sides
d. six sides
e. two equal sides

C-2

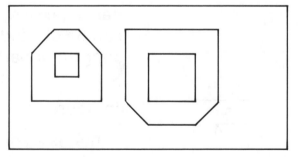

Each figure contains:

a. a four-sided figure
b. a five-sided figure
c. a six-sided figure
d. ten lines
e. a shape within a shape

C-3

Each figure is:

a. all white
b. half white
c. a square
d. a rectangle

CLASSIFICATIONS

DESCRIBING CLASSES

Circle the letter in front of each statement that is true.

C-4

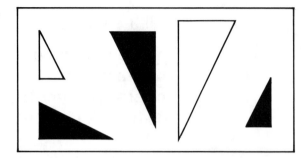

All the figures are:

a. the same color
b. congruent
c. similar
d. right triangles

C-5

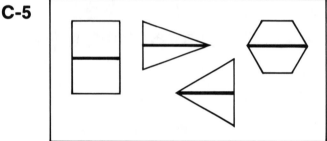

Each figure:

a. is the same shape
b. has a stripe
c. is a regular polygon*
d. has an axis of symmetry
e. has more than one axis of symmetry

C-6

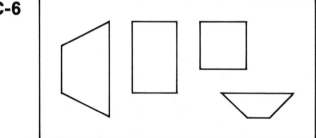

Each figure:

a. has four sides
b. has a right angle
c. is irregular
d. has an axis of symmetry
e. can be divided into two congruent parts

C-7

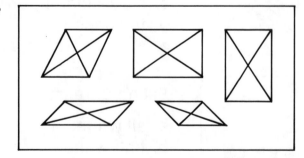

Each figure:

a. contains a square
b. has two pair of parallel sides
c. has six lines
d. contains a rectangle

*A regular polygon is a many-sided figure having equal sides and equal angles.

MATCHING CLASSES

Draw lines between boxes that contain shapes which belong to the same class.

EXAMPLE:

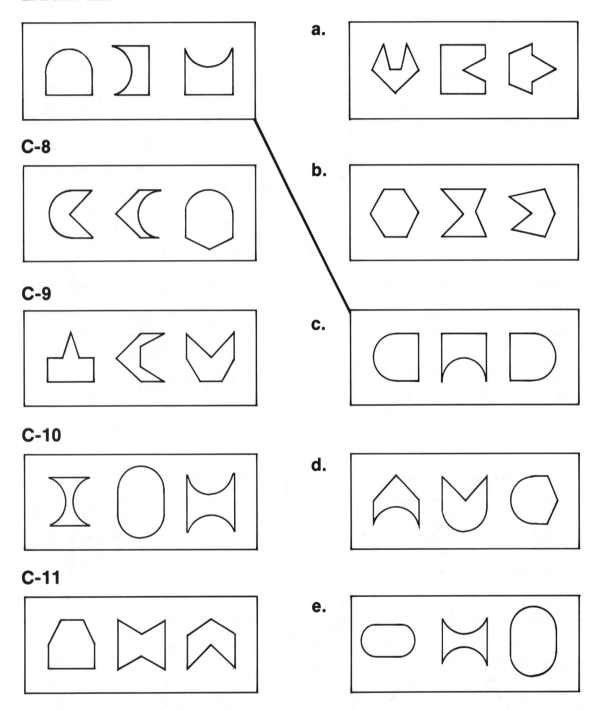

C-8

C-9

C-10

C-11

CLASSIFICATIONS

MATCHING CLASSES

Draw lines between boxes that contain shapes which belong to the same class.

C-12
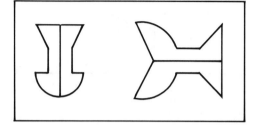

a.
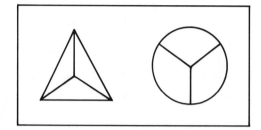

C-13
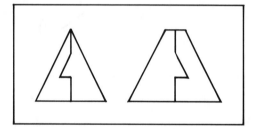

b.
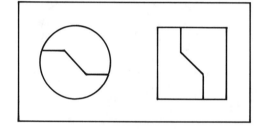

C-14
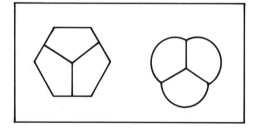

c.
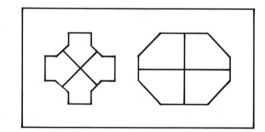

C-15
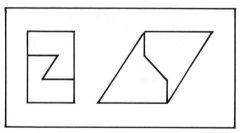

d.
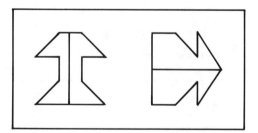

C-16
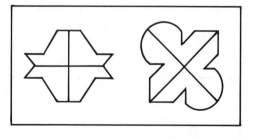

e.
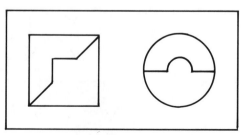

CLASSIFYING MORE THAN ONE WAY—MATCHING

Match the figure at the left to all the classes to which it can belong. You can match the figure by one or more characteristics.

For example, can belong to class f (hexagons)

or classes b or e (white figures). Write the letters of ALL the classes to which it can belong on the line next to each figure.

EXAMPLE:

  f, b, e

C-17   _____

C-18   _____

C-19   _____

C-20   _____

C-21   _____

C-22   _____

a.

b.

c.

d.

e.

f.

CLASSIFICATIONS

CLASSIFYING MORE THAN ONE WAY—MATCHING

Match the figure at the left to all the classes to which it can belong. You can match the figure by one or more characteristics. Write the letters of ALL the classes to which it can belong on the line next to each figure.

C-23 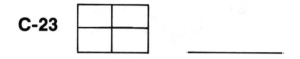 _____   **a.**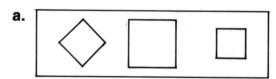

C-24 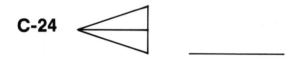 _____   **b.**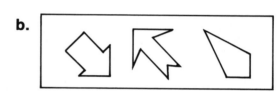

C-25 _____   **c.**

C-26 _____   **d.**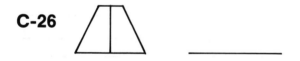

C-27 _____   **e.**

C-28  _____   **f.**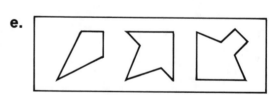

C-29 _____   **g.**

© 1985 MIDWEST PUBLICATIONS 93950

CLASSIFYING MORE THAN ONE WAY—MATCHING

Match the figure at the left to all the classes to which it can belong. You can match the figure by one or more characteristics. Write the letters of ALL the classes to which it can belong on the line next to each figure.

C-30 _____

C-31 _____

C-32 _____

C-33 _____

C-34 _____

C-35 _____

C-36 _____

C-37 _____

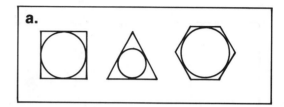

a.

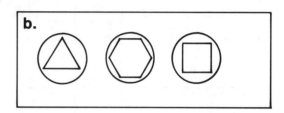

b.

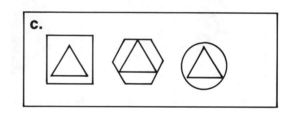

c.

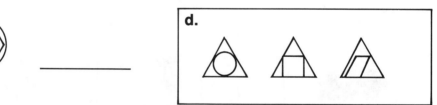

d.

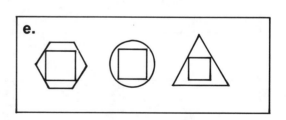

e.

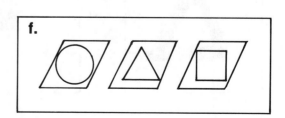

f.

CLASSIFICATIONS

CHANGING CHARACTERISTICS—SELECT

Look at each pair of figures below. In the answer column, circle **S** if the characteristic is the same for both figures. Circle **D** if the characteristic is different.

EXAMPLE:

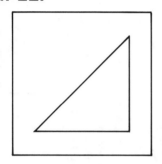 

ANSWERS:

Size	S	Ⓓ
Shape	Ⓢ	D
Pattern	S	Ⓓ
Direction	S	Ⓓ

C-38

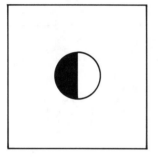 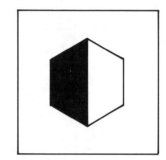

Size	S	D
Shape	S	D
Pattern	S	D

C-39

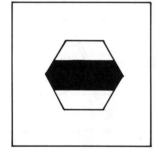 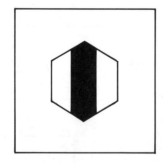

Size	S	D
Shape	S	D
Pattern	S	D
Direction	S	D

C-40

 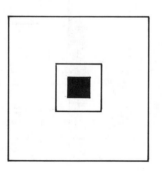

Size	S	D
Shape	S	D
Pattern	S	D

CHANGING CHARACTERISTICS—SELECT

Look at each pair of figures below. In the answer column, circle **S** if the characteristic is the same for both figures. Circle **D** if the characteristic is different.

C-41

 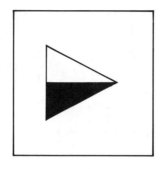

ANSWERS:

Size	S	D
Shape	S	D
Pattern	S	D
Direction	S	D

C-42

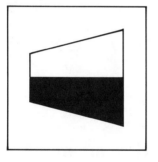 

Size	S	D
Shape	S	D
Pattern	S	D
Direction	S	D

C-43

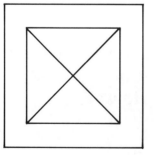 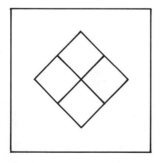

Size	S	D
Shape	S	D
Pattern	S	D
Direction	S	D

C-44

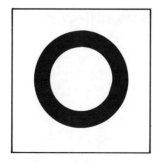 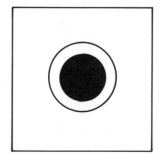

Size	S	D
Shape	S	D
Pattern	S	D

CLASSIFICATIONS

DESCRIBING CHARACTERISTICS

Examine each pair of shapes. Describe how each shape in the pair is alike and how it is different from the other shape.

EXAMPLE:

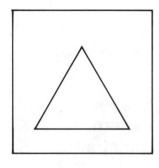 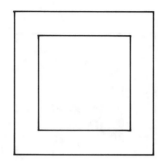

How alike?

Both have all sides equal*
Both have all angles equal**
Equal bases

How different?

Square has four sides
Square has a greater height

C-45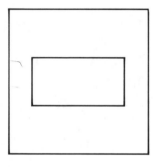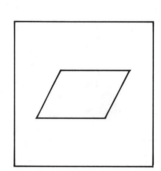

How alike?

How different?

C-46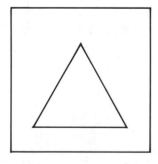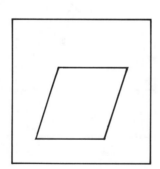

How alike?

How different?

*equilateral

**equiangular

200

DESCRIBING CHARACTERISTICS

Examine each pair of shapes. Describe how each shape in the pair is alike and how it is different from the other shape.

C-47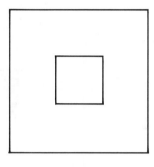

How alike?

How different?

C-48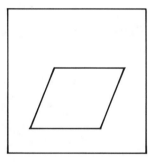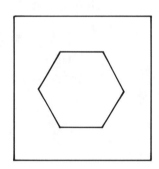

How alike?

How different?

C-49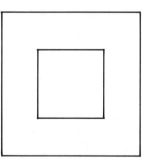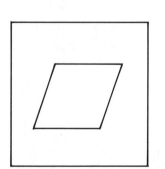

How alike?

How different?

CLASSIFICATIONS

CHANGING CHARACTERISTICS—SUPPLY

Look at the figure on the left. Read the directions and then draw another figure with the characteristics described in the directions.

EXAMPLE: **ANSWER:**

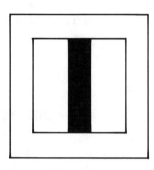

Directions

Keep the shape and pattern the same. Decrease the size.

C-50

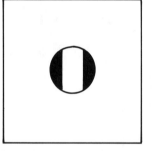

Directions

Keep the shape and pattern the same. Increase the size.

C-51

Directions

Keep the size and shape the same. Reverse the pattern.

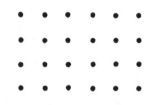

C-52

Directions

Keep the size, shape, and pattern the same. Change the direction.

© 1985 MIDWEST PUBLICATIONS 93950

CHANGING CHARACTERISTICS—SUPPLY

Look at the figure on the left. Read the directions and then draw another figure with the characteristics described in the directions.

C-53

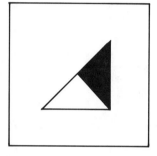

Directions

Keep the shape and pattern the same. Increase size and rotate one position to the right.

C-54

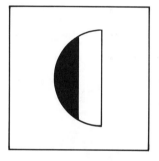

Directions

Keep the size the same. Reflect about the vertical axis and reverse the pattern.

C-55

Directions

Keep the size the same. Reflect about the horizontal axis and reverse the pattern.

C-56

Directions

Keep the shape and pattern the same. Reduce the size and rotate one position to the left.

CLASSIFICATIONS

DRAW ANOTHER

For each group below, draw another figure with the same characteristics.

C-57

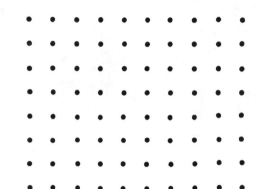

C-58

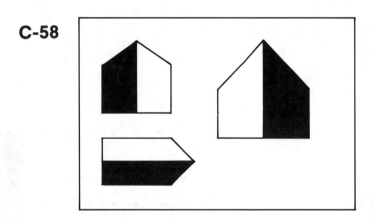

C-59

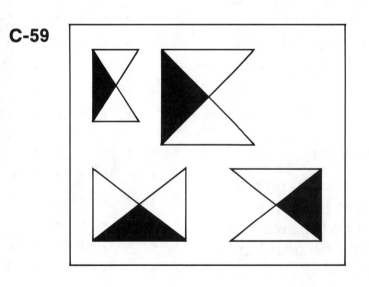

DRAW ANOTHER

For each group below, draw another figure with the same characteristics.

C-60

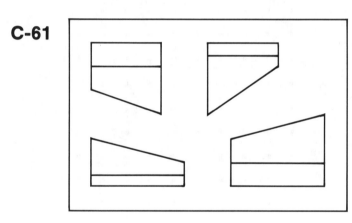

C-61

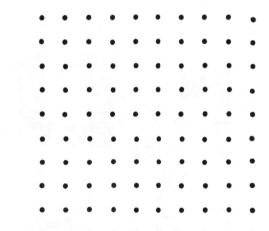

C-62

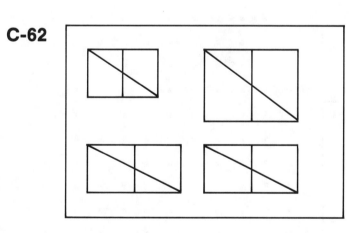

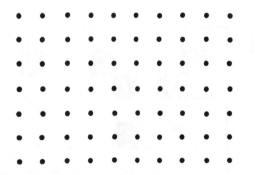

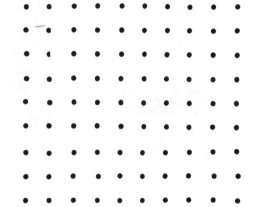

DRAW ANOTHER

For each group below, draw another figure with the same characteristics.

C-63

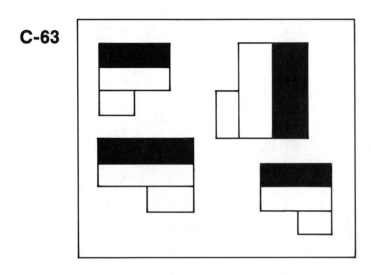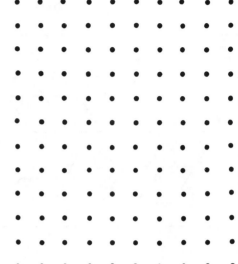

C-64

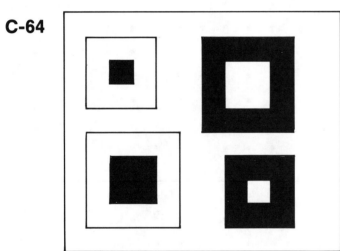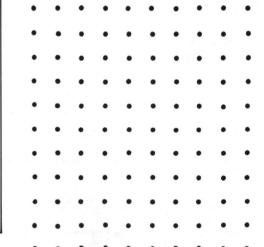

C-65

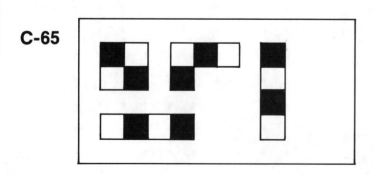

DRAW ANOTHER

For each group below, draw another figure with the same characteristics.

C-66

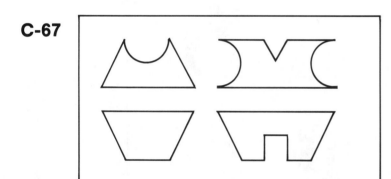

C-67

C-68

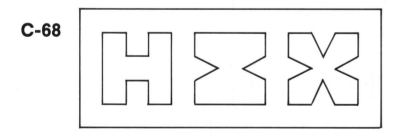

C-69

CLASSIFICATIONS

CLASSIFYING BY PATTERN—SORTING

Sort this collection of figures by pattern. Below each figure is a number. Put the number for each figure in the correct sorting box. The sorting boxes each contain an example to show the kind of pattern belonging in the box.

C-70

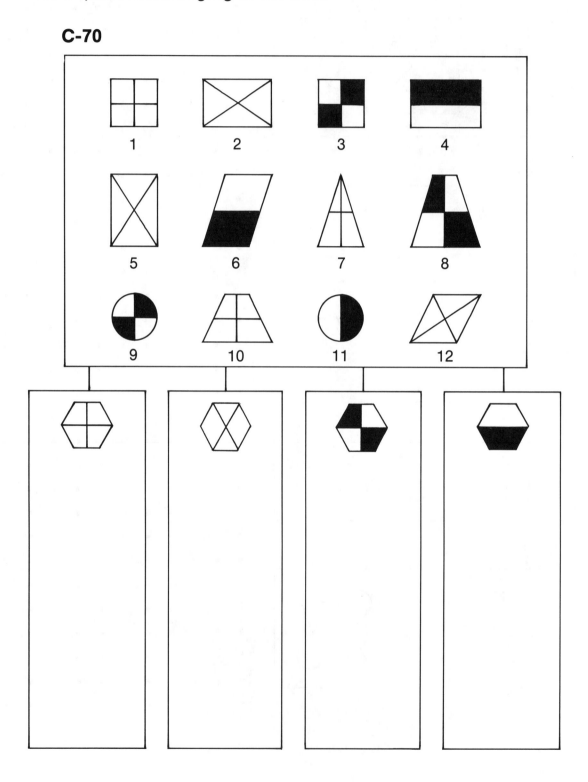

CLASSIFYING MORE THAN ONE WAY—SORTING

Sort this collection by putting the number for each figure in the correct classification box. Each of the figures can be classified more than one way, and you will need to use all the numbers more than once.

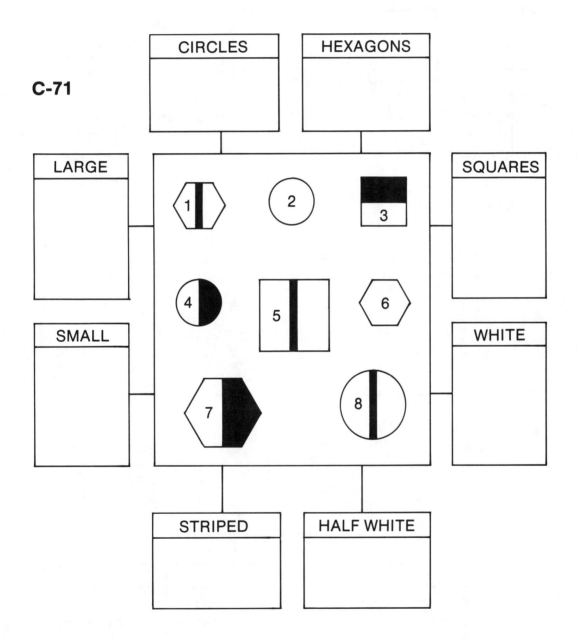

CIRCLES

HEXAGONS

C-71

LARGE

SQUARES

SMALL

WHITE

STRIPED

HALF WHITE

© 1985 MIDWEST PUBLICATIONS 93950

CLASSIFYING BY SHAPE—SORTING

Sort this collection of figures by shape. Below each figure is a number. Put the figure number or draw each figure in the correct sorting box.

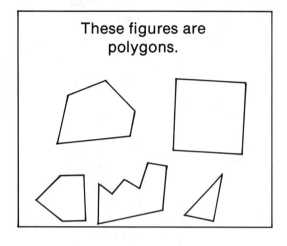

These figures are polygons.

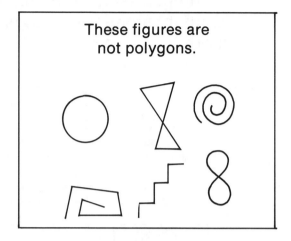

These figures are not polygons.

C-72

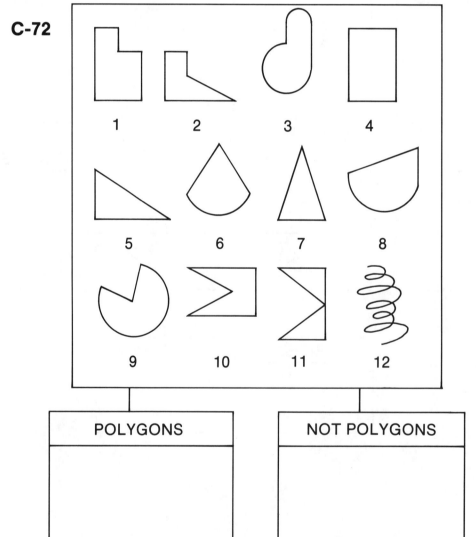

POLYGONS

NOT POLYGONS

CLASSIFYING BY SHAPE—SORTING

Examine the same collection of figures and sort them according to whether they are symmetrical or not symmetrical. Put the figure number or draw the figure in the correct sorting box.

C-73

Symmetrical	Not Symmetrical

CLASSIFICATIONS

CLASSIFYING BY SHAPE — SORTING

Examine the same collection of figures and sort them into classes and subclasses. Decide on the characteristic for the first stage of classification. Label the sorting boxes and sort the figures accordingly. Then subdivide each class into subclasses. Label the sorting boxes and sort each subclass accordingly. Put the figure number or draw each figure in the correct sorting box.

C-74

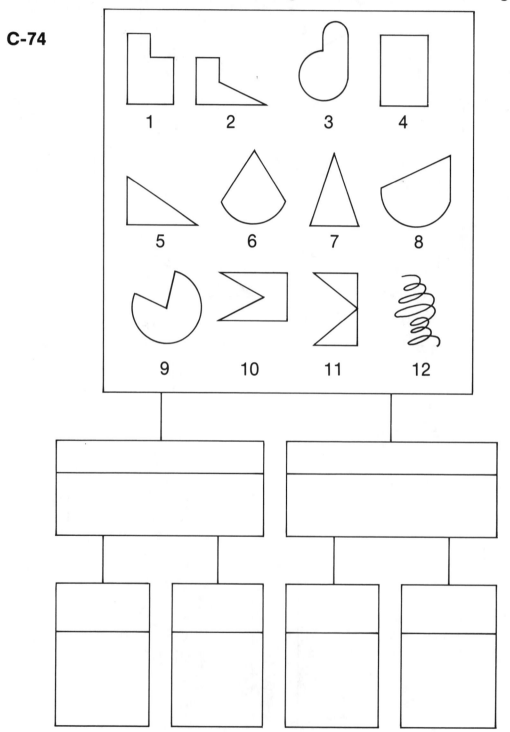

© 1985 MIDWEST PUBLICATIONS 93950

DISCOVERING CLASSES

Examine this collection of figures. Decide how to divide this group into two classes. Label the classes and put the number for each figure in the correct sorting box. All the figures must be used.

C-75

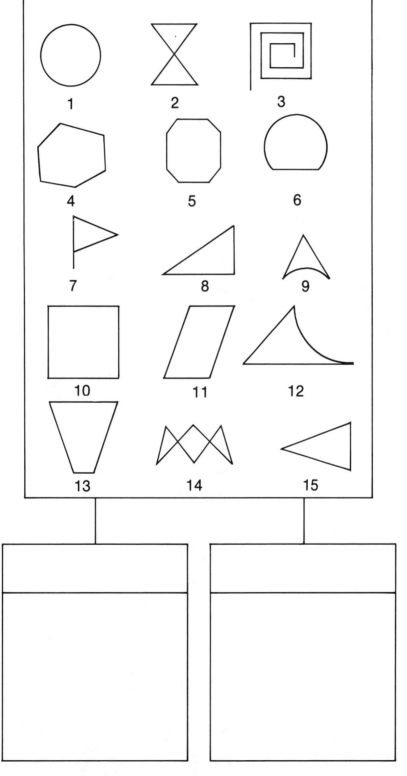

CLASSIFICATIONS

DISCOVERING CLASSES

Examine this collection of figures again. Find another characteristic by which this group can be divided into two groups. Label the classes and put the number for each figure in the correct sorting box.

C-76

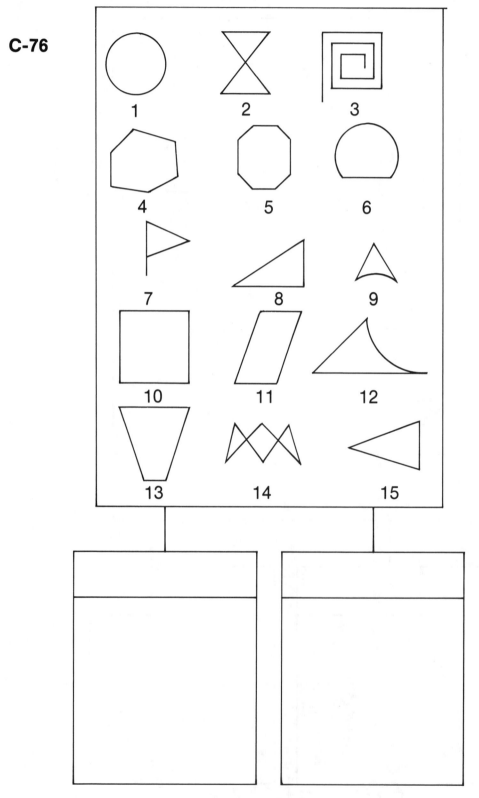

© 1985 MIDWEST PUBLICATIONS 93950

DISCOVERING CLASSES

You have sorted this collection of figures by two characteristics. To organize the figures by both characteristics, select one of the characteristics and sort the figures into two classes. Divide each class into two subclasses. Label the classes and put the number for each figure in the correct sorting box.

C-77

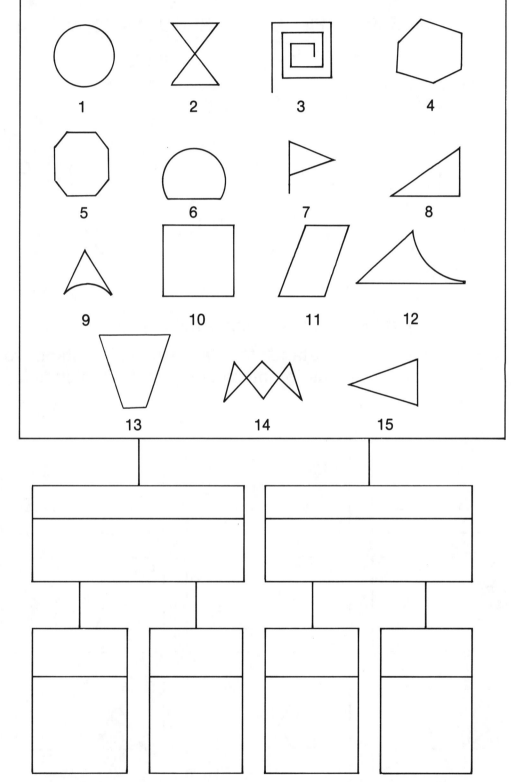

CLASSIFICATIONS

OVERLAPPING CLASSES—INTERSECTIONS

An overlapping-classes diagram (called a Venn diagram) can be used to show the relationship between two classes if some, but not all, of the characteristics are shared by both classes. Recall that a regular polygon has all its sides the same length.

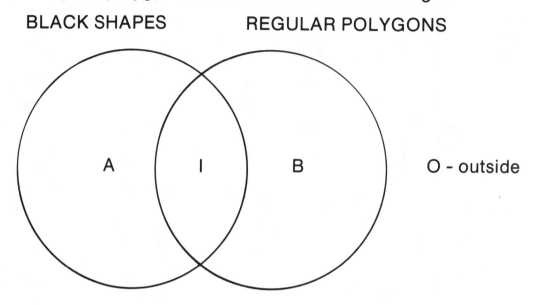

BLACK SHAPES　　　　REGULAR POLYGONS

A　　I　　B　　　　O - outside

Where do each of the following shapes belong?

(Answer A, B, I, or O. "A" stands for black shape, "B" stands for regular polygon, "I" stands for intersection, and "O" stands for outside.)

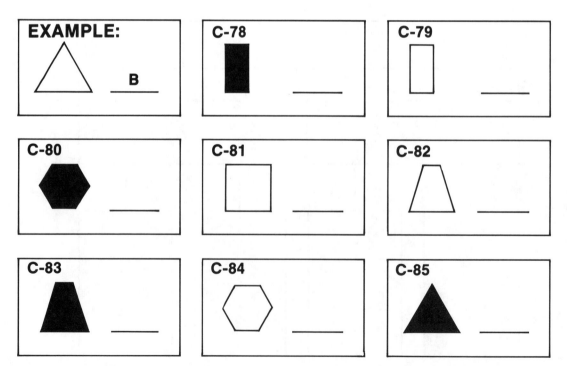

EXAMPLE: ____B____

C-78 ____

C-79 ____

C-80 ____

C-81 ____

C-82 ____

C-83 ____

C-84 ____

C-85 ____

OVERLAPPING CLASSES—INTERSECTIONS

An overlapping-classes diagram (called a Venn diagram) can be used to show the relationship between two classes if some, but not all, of the characteristics are shared by both classes.

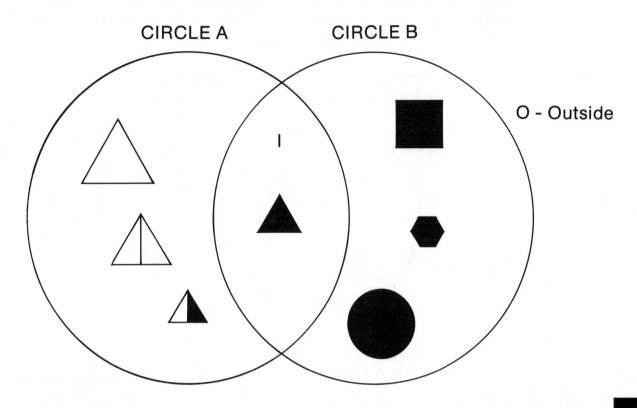

C-86 Circle A contains the class _____

C-87 Circle B contains the class _____

C-88 The intersection contains the class _____

Where do each of the following shapes belong?

(Answer A, B, I, or O. "A" stands for circle A, "B" stands for circle B, "I" stands for intersection, and "O" stands for outside.)

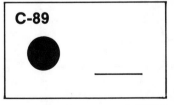

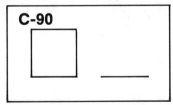

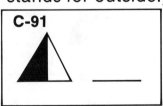

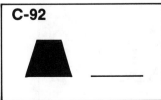

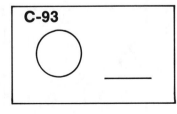

CLASSIFICATIONS

OVERLAPPING CLASSES—INTERSECTIONS

An overlapping-classes diagram (called a Venn diagram) can be used to show the relationship between two classes if some, but not all, of the characteristics are shared by both classes.

Examine this Venn diagram. From the location of the figures, determine the characteristics of each class.

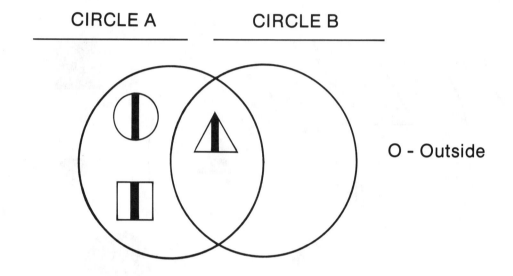

CIRCLE A   CIRCLE B

O - Outside

C-95   Circle A contains the class _____

C-96   Circle B contains the class _____

Where do each of the following shapes belong?

(Answer A, B, I, or O. "A" stands for circle A, "B" stands for circle B, "I" stands for the intersection, "O" stands for outside.)

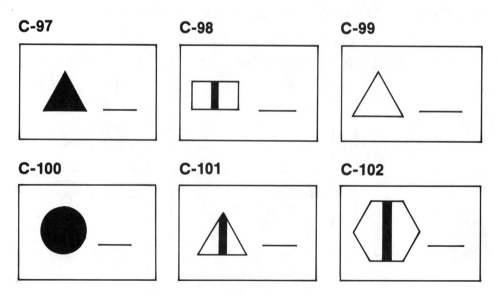

C-97   **C-98**   **C-99**

C-100   **C-101**   **C-102**

OVERLAPPING CLASSES—INTERSECTIONS

It is possible to classify figures by a characteristic that they **do not** have, such as "not striped" and "not-regular polygons." Recall that a regular polygon has all its sides the same length.

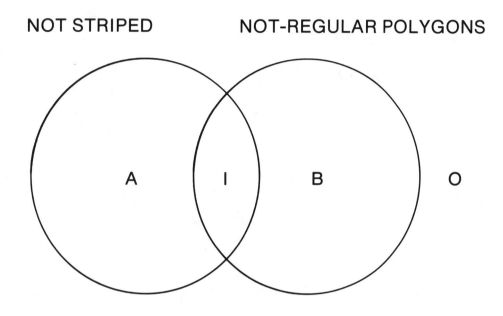

NOT STRIPED   NOT-REGULAR POLYGONS

A   I   B   O

Where do each of the following shapes belong?

(Answer A, B, I, or O. "A" stands for not striped, "B" stands for not-regular polygon, "I" stands for the intersection, and "O" stands for outside.)

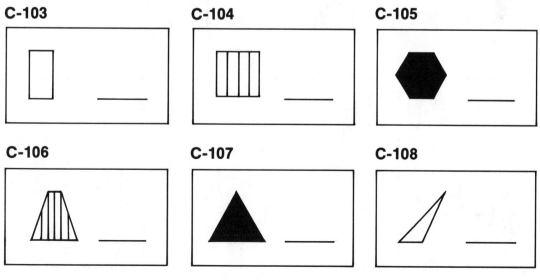

C-103   C-104   C-105

C-106   C-107   C-108

CLASSIFICATIONS

OVERLAPPING CLASSES—INTERSECTIONS

An overlapping-classes diagram (called a Venn diagram) can be used to show the relationship between classes if some, but not all, of the characteristics are shared by two or three classes.

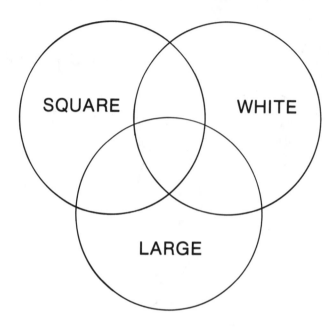

Darken the region of each small Venn diagram in which each figure fits.

EXAMPLE:

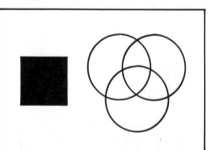

C-109

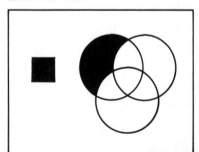

C-110

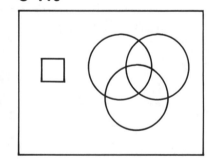

C-111

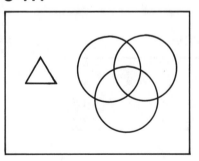

C-112

C-113

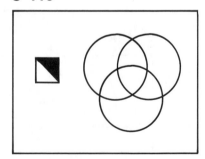

OVERLAPPING CLASSES—INTERSECTIONS

An overlapping-classes diagram (called a Venn diagram) can be used to show the relationship between classes if some, but not all, of the characteristics are shared by two or three classes.

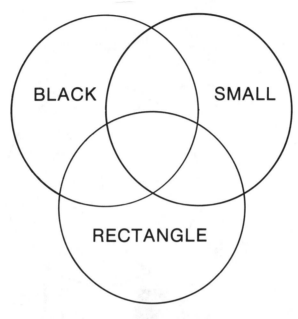

Darken the region of each small Venn diagram in which each figure belongs.

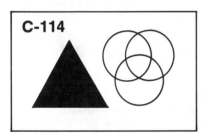

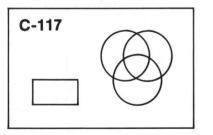

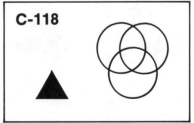

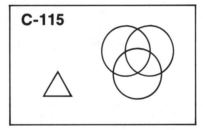

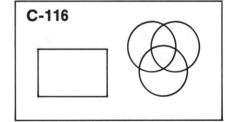

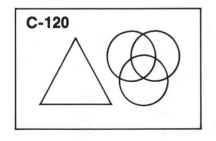

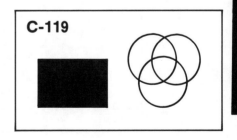

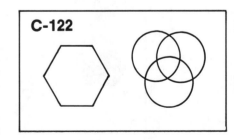

CLASSIFICATIONS

OVERLAPPING CLASSES—INTERSECTIONS

Examine the Venn diagram. From the location of the figures, determine the characteristics of each class. Label each circle.

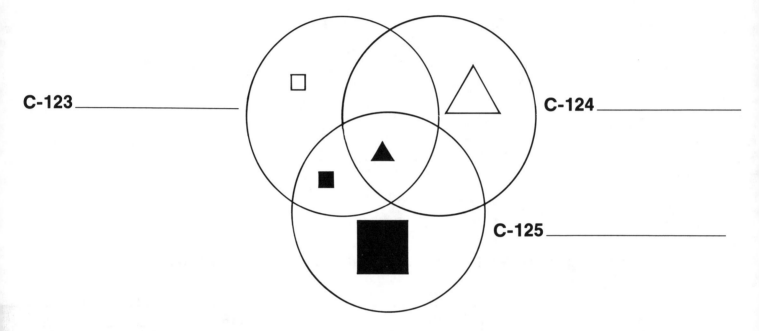

Darken the region of each small Venn diagram in which each figure belongs.

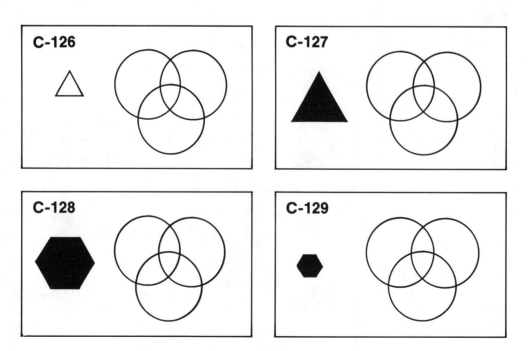

© 1985 MIDWEST PUBLICATIONS 93950

OVERLAPPING CLASSES—INTERSECTIONS

Examine the Venn diagram. From the location of the figures, determine the characteristics of each class. Label each circle.

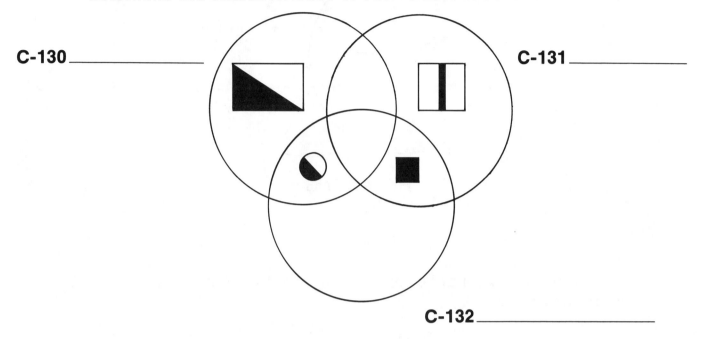

C-130 _____

C-131 _____

C-132 _____

Darken the region of each small Venn diagram in which each figure belongs.

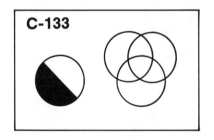

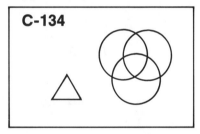

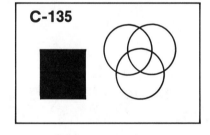

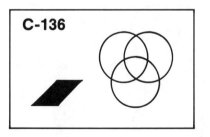

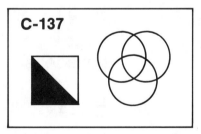

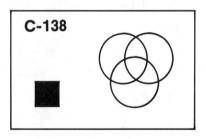

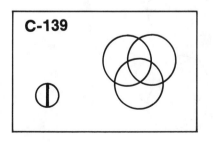

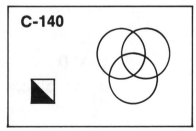

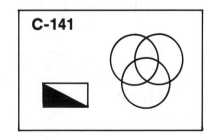

CLASSIFICATIONS

OVERLAPPING CLASSES—INTERSECTIONS

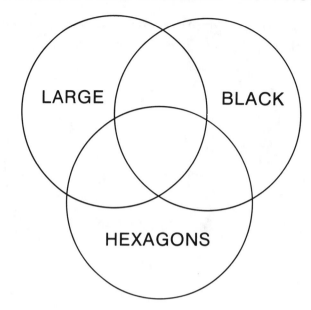

Darken the region described for each of the small Venn diagrams below.

EXAMPLE:
Small, black squares

C-142
large, white hexagons

C-143
black hexagons

C-144
large, white triangles

C-145
small, black hexagons

C-146
large, black rectangles

C-147
small, white hexagons

C-148
large hexagons

C-149
large, black hexagons

C-150
large, black figures

OVERLAPPING CIRCLES—INTERSECTIONS

An overlapping-classes diagram (called a Venn diagram) can be used to show relationships between or among classes if some, but not all, of the characteristics are shared by two or three classes. It is possible to classify figures by a characteristic they **do not** have, such as "not square" or "not white."

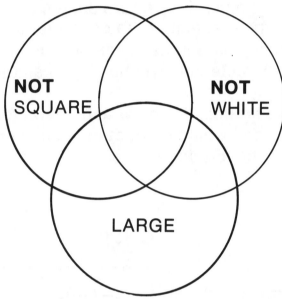

Darken the region described for each of the small Venn diagrams below.

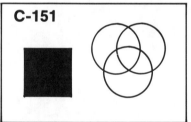

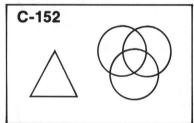

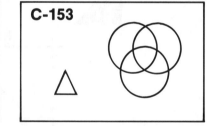

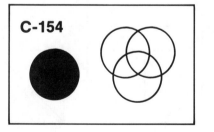

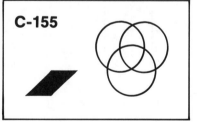

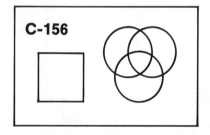

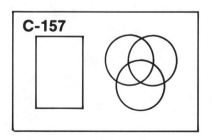

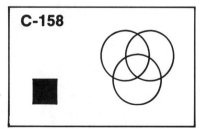

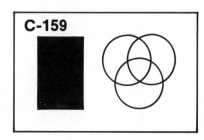

CLASSIFICATIONS

OVERLAPPING CLASSES—MATRIX

A matrix diagram can be used to organize a group of objects to describe their characteristics in more than one way. All the objects in a row must have the same characteristic, and all the objects in a column must have another characteristic.

Note: Rows go across and columns go up and down.

In each box of the matrix, a figure shares two characteristics. For example, in the first matrix the characteristics are pattern and direction. One characteristic will be true of all the figures in a row; the other characteristic will be true of all the figures in a column.

Using the clue figures, decide which characteristic must be true of each row and which characteristic must be true of each column. Draw in the missing figures.

C-161

C-160

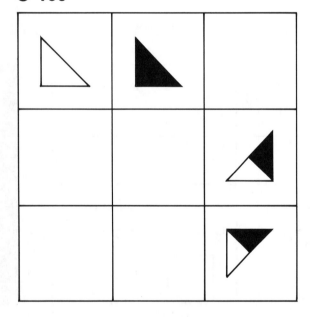

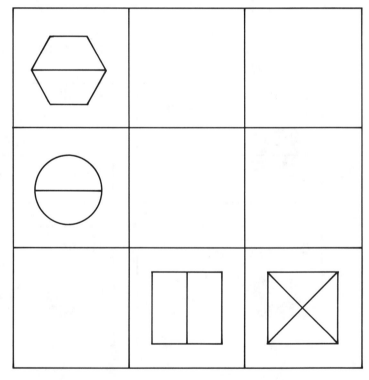

OVERLAPPING CLASSES—MATRIX

Complete each matrix.

C-162

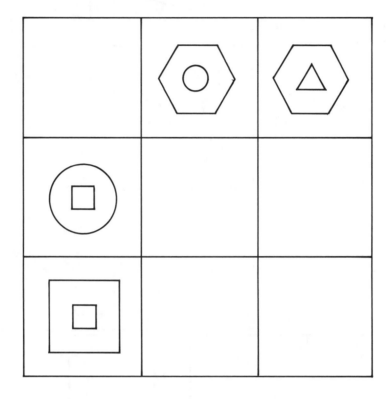

C-163

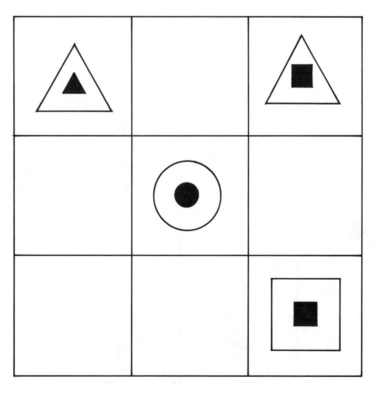

CLASSIFICATIONS

OVERLAPPING CLASSES— MATRIX

Complete each matrix.

C-164

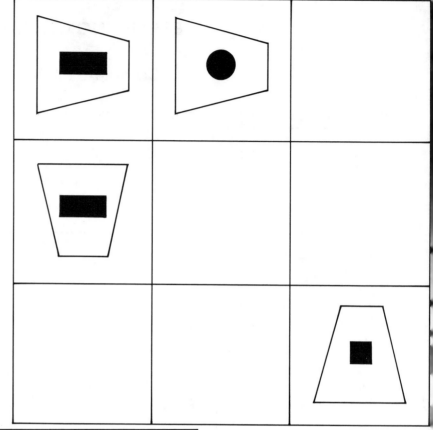

C-165

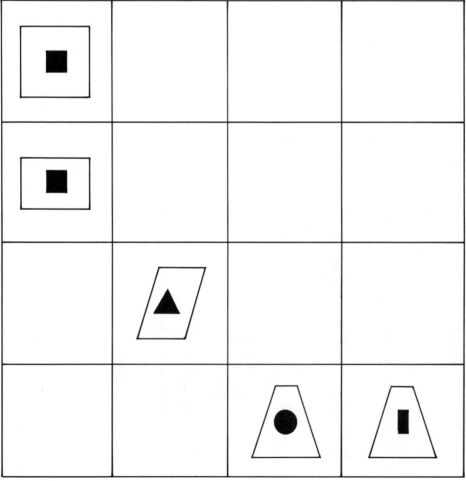

© 1985 MIDWEST PUBLICATIONS 93950

DEDUCE THE CLASS

In the next group of exercises, you will continue to classify figures; but now you must determine the characteristics of the class. Look at the figures that belong to the class. Look at the figures that do **not** belong to that class.

By looking at the sample figures for each problem, decide what is true of the members of the group or class. You may wish to look at the number of straight lines and the number of curved lines in each figure.

After you have decided (deduced) the characteristics of the class, decide whether other figures belong to that class.

HERE ARE THE STEPS:

1. Carefully study the figures.

2. Decide (deduce) what the characteristics of the class are by asking yourself these questions:

   How are the figures in the class alike?

   How are the figures that are **not** in the class different from those that **are** in the class?

3. Look at the figures in the questions and decide if they belong in the class.

CLASSIFICATIONS

DEDUCE THE CLASS

"BITRIS"

Use the six clue figures to deduce what a "bitri" is.

These figures are bitris.	These figures are **not** bitris.
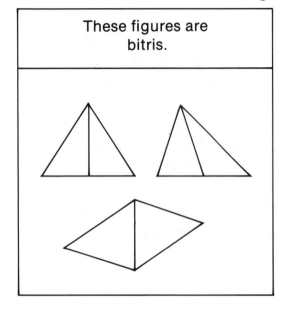	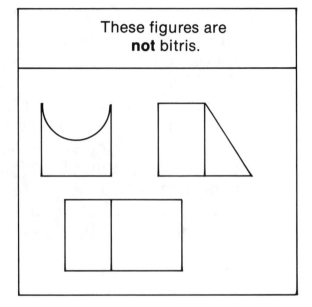

For each of the following figures, answer **Yes** or **No** on the line near each figure.

Are these figures bitris?

EXAMPLE:

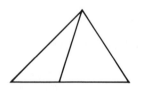 Answer ___yes___

C-166

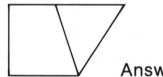 Answer _____

C-167

 Answer _____

C-168

 Answer _____

C-169

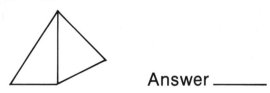 Answer _____

C-170

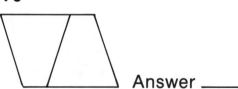 Answer _____

© 1985 MIDWEST PUBLICATIONS 93950

DEDUCE THE CLASS

"BIQUADS"

Use the six clue figures to deduce what a "biquad" is.

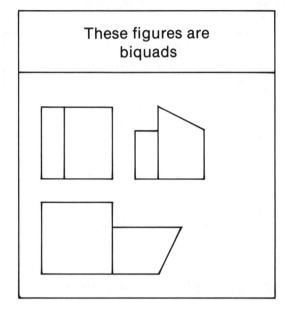

These figures are biquads

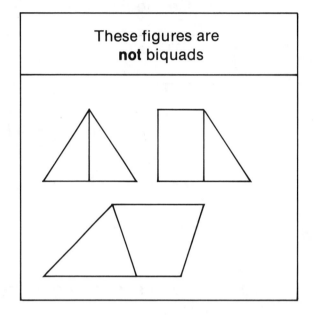

These figures are **not** biquads

For each of the following figures, answer **Yes** or **No** on the line near each figure.

Are these figures biquads?

C-171

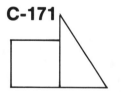

Answer _____

C-172

Answer _____

C-173

Answer _____

C-174

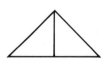

Answer _____

C-175

Answer _____

C-176

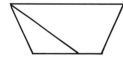

Answer _____

CLASSIFICATIONS

DEDUCE THE CLASS

"BILINCIRCS"

Use the five clue figures to deduce what a "bilincirc" is.

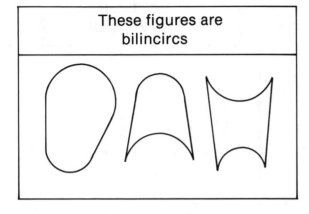

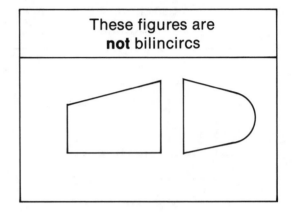

For each of the following figures, answer **Yes** or **No** on the line near each figure.

Are these figures bilincircs?

C-177

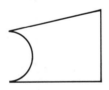

Answer _____

C-178

Answer _____

C-179

Answer _____

C-180

Answer _____

C-181

Answer _____

C-182

Answer _____

© 1985 MIDWEST PUBLICATIONS 93950

FIGURAL ANALOGIES—SELECT
Circle the figure that completes each figural analogy.

EXAMPLE: **ANSWER:**

 : 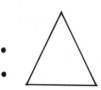 ::  :

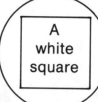

A black   is to   a white   as   a black   is to
triangle   triangle   square

D-1

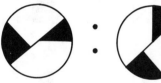 ::

a.   **b.**

c.   **d.**

D-2

 :  :: :

a.   **b.**

c.   **d.**

ANALOGIES

FIGURAL ANALOGIES—SELECT

Circle the figure that completes each figural analogy.

D-3

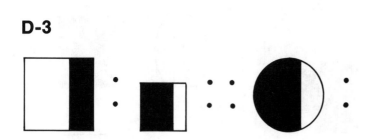

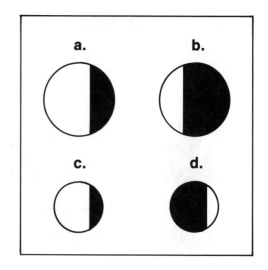

D-4

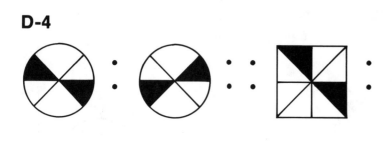

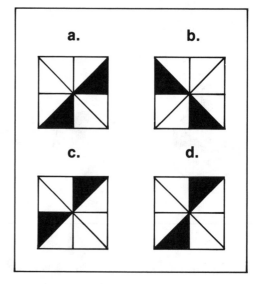

D-5

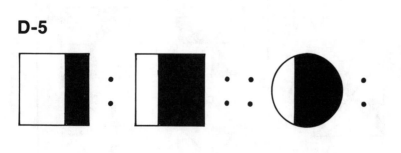

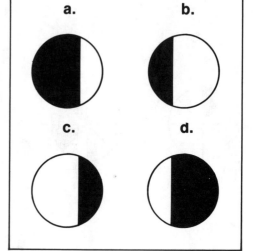

FIGURAL ANALOGIES—SELECT

Select the figure that completes the analogy. Write the letter for the correct figure on the line provided.

A : B :: C : D

CHOICE BOX

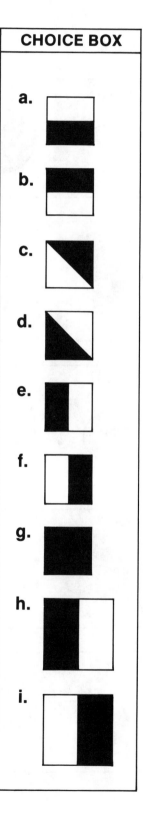

EXAMPLE:

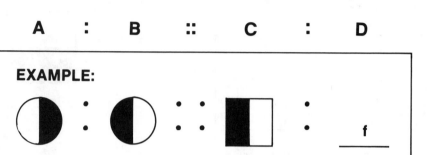

D-6

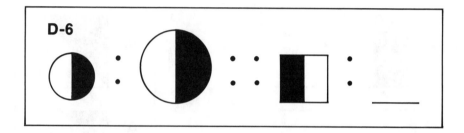

D-7

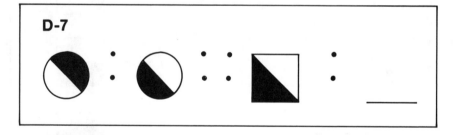

D-8

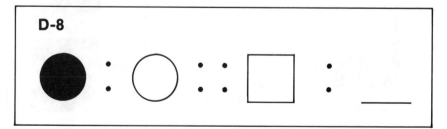

D-9

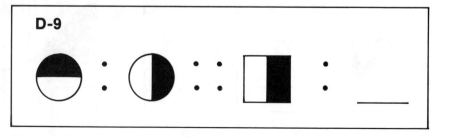

ANALOGIES

FIGURAL ANALOGIES—SELECT

Select the figure that completes the analogy. Write the letter for the correct figure on the line provided.

A　:　B　::　C　:　D

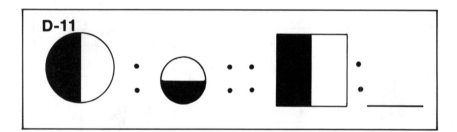

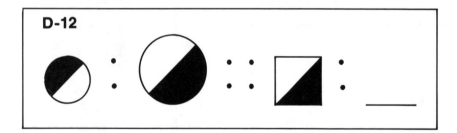

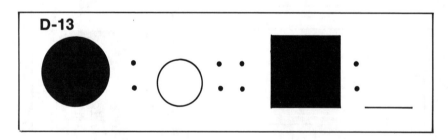

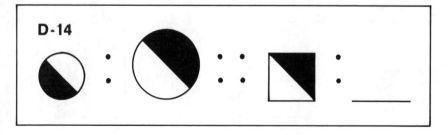

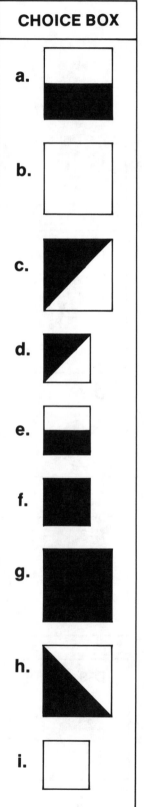

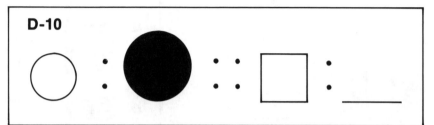

FIGURAL ANALOGIES—SELECT

Select the figure that completes the analogy. Write the letter for the correct figure on the line provided.

A : B :: C : D

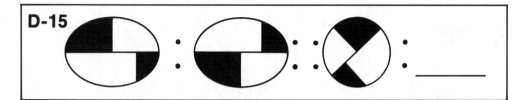

D-15

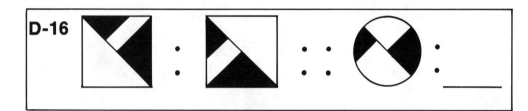

D-16

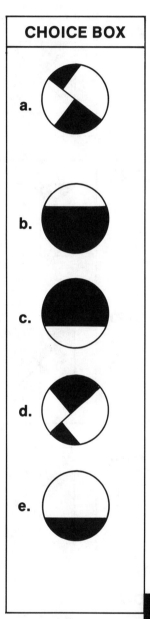

CHOICE BOX

a.

b.

c.

d.

e.

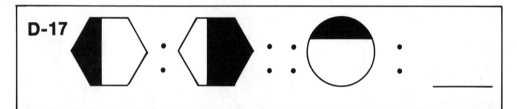

D-17

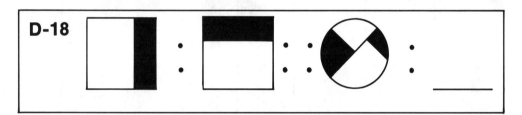

D-18

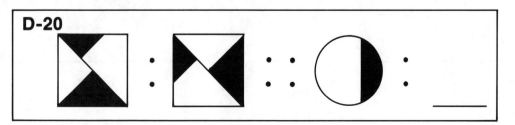

D-19

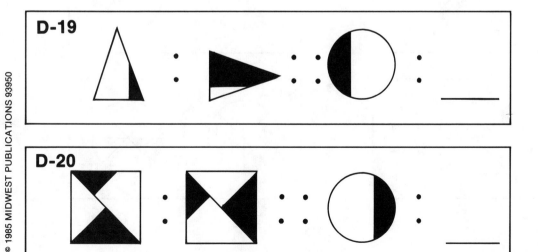

D-20

© 1985 MIDWEST PUBLICATIONS 93950

ANALOGIES

FIGURAL ANALOGIES—SELECT A PAIR

Draw lines between the pairs that correctly form an analogy
(A : B :: C : D). Remember, in an analogy, both pairs must be
related in the same way.

A   :   B   ::   C   :   D

D-21 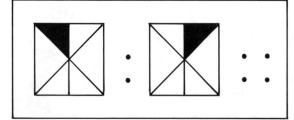   **a.**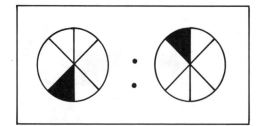

D-22 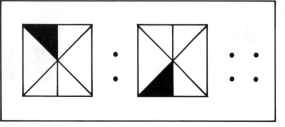   **b.**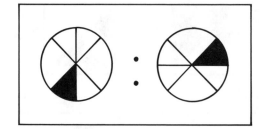

D-23 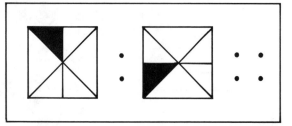   **c.**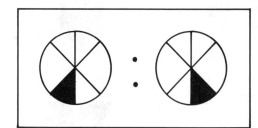

D-24 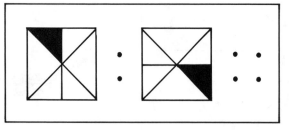   **d.**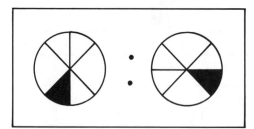

D-25 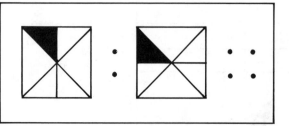   **e.**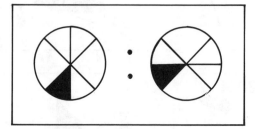

© 1985 MIDWEST PUBLICATIONS 93950

FIGURAL ANALOGIES—SELECT A PAIR

Draw lines between the pairs that correctly form an analogy
(A : B :: C : D). Remember, in an analogy, both pairs must be
related in the same way.

A   :   B   ::   C   :   D

D-26

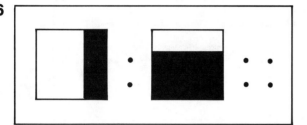

a.

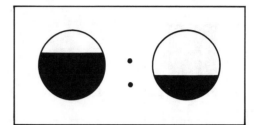

D-27

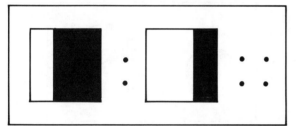

b.

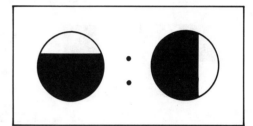

D-28

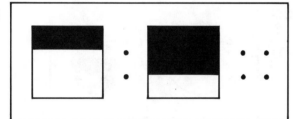

c.

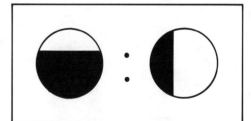

D-29

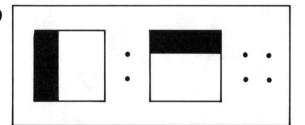

d.

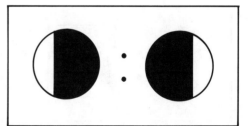

D-30

e.

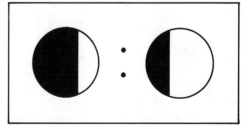

ANALOGIES

FIGURAL ANALOGIES—SELECT A PAIR

Draw lines between the pairs that correctly form an analogy
(A : B :: C : D). Remember, in an analogy, both pairs must be
related in the same way.

A　　:　　B　　::　　　　C　　:　　D

D-31
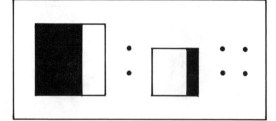
　　　　　　　　　　　　　a.
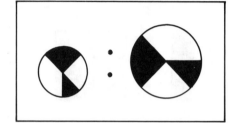

D-32
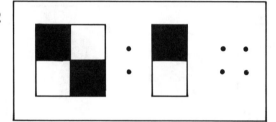
　　　　　　　　　　　　　b.
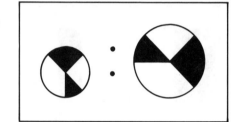

D-33
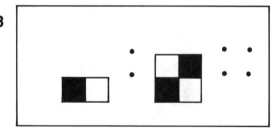
　　　　　　　　　　　　　c.
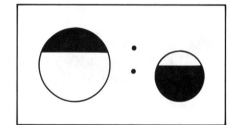

D-34
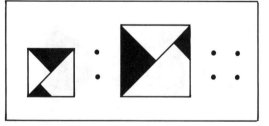
　　　　　　　　　　　　　d.
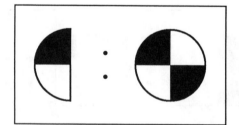

D-35
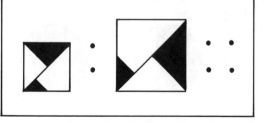
　　　　　　　　　　　　　e.
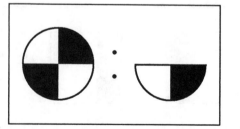

DESCRIBING TYPES OF FIGURAL ANALOGIES

In the exercises you have just done, there are several types of relationships. These relationships can be described as follows:

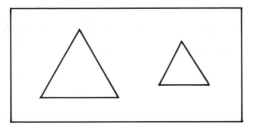

SIZE
(example shows a
decrease in size)

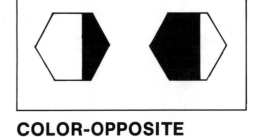

COLOR-OPPOSITE

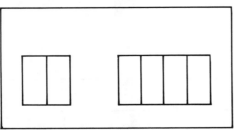

DETAIL or PARTS
(example shows an
increase in number
of parts)

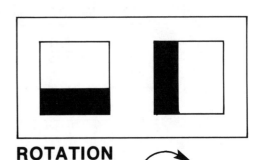

ROTATION
(to the right)

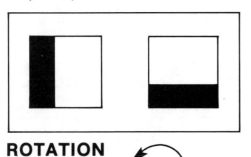

ROTATION
(to the left)

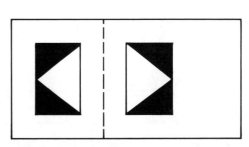

REFLECTION
(about a vertical line)

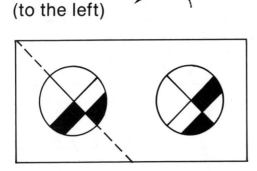

REFLECTION
(about a diagonal line)

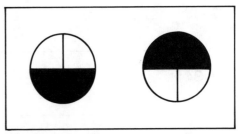

REFLECTION
(about a horizontal line)

ANALOGIES

DESCRIBING TYPES OF FIGURAL ANALOGIES

Look back at the figural analogies **D-26** through **D-35** on pages 239 and 240. Name the relationships that fit each of these analogies.

D-26   **EXAMPLE:** Rotate one-quarter turn to the left

and color opposite.

D-27 _____

_____

D-28 _____

_____

D-29 _____

_____

D-30 _____

_____

D-31 _____

_____

D-32 _____

_____

D-33 _____

_____

D-34 _____

_____

D-35 _____

_____

COMPLETE THE PAIR

On the grid in each box, draw a figure that illustrates the relationship written below the box.

EXAMPLE:

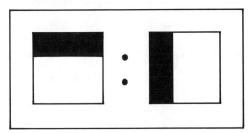

Rotate one position
to the left.

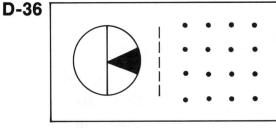

D-36

Reflect about the
vertical line.

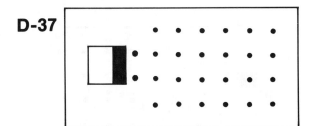

D-37

Increase size and rotate
one position to the right.

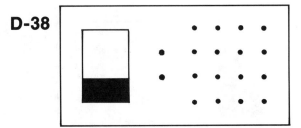

D-38

Rotate one position to
the left and color
opposite.

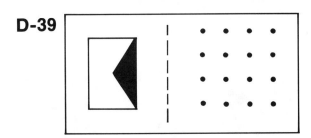

D-39

Reduce size and reflect
about the vertical line.

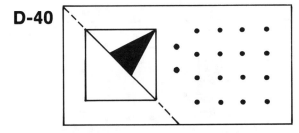

D-40

Reduce size and reflect
about the diagonal line.

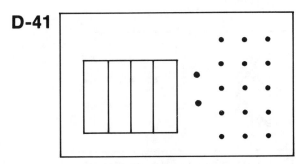

D-41

Reduce the number
of parts.

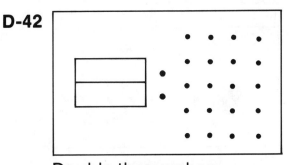

D-42

Double the number
of parts.

ANALOGIES

COMPLETE THE PAIR

On the grid in each box, draw a figure that illustrates the relationship written below the box.

D-43

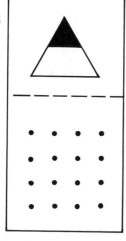

Reflect about the horizontal and color opposite.

D-44

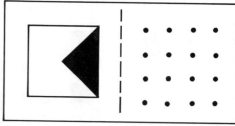

Reflect about the vertical and color opposite.

D-45

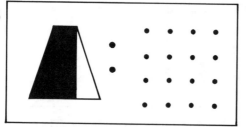

Rotate quarter turn to the left and decrease size.

D-46

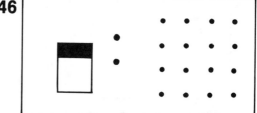

Increase size and rotate one position to the right.

D-47

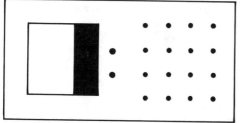

Decrease size and reflect about the vertical.

D-48

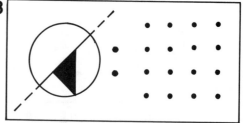

Reflect about the diagonal.

D-49

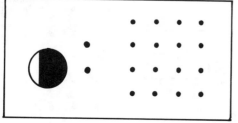

Color opposite and increase size.

D-50

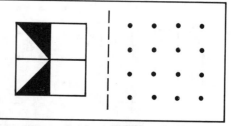

Reflect about the vertical and reduce the size.

FIGURAL ANALOGIES—SUPPLY

On the grid of dots, draw in the figures that will complete these figural analogies.

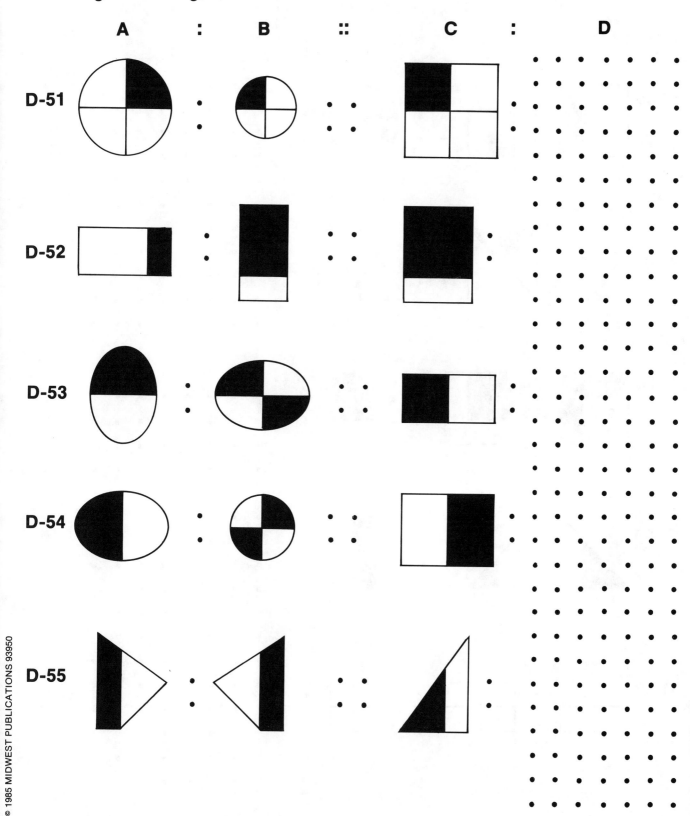

A : B :: C : D

D-51

D-52

D-53

D-54

D-55

ANALOGIES

FIGURAL ANALOGIES—SUPPLY
On the grid of dots, draw in the figures that will complete these figural analogies.

A : **B** :: **C** : **D**

D-56

D-57

D-58

D-59

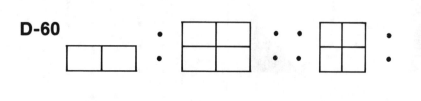

D-60

FIGURAL ANALOGIES—SUPPLY
On the grid of dots, draw in the figures that will complete these figural analogies.

A : B :: C : D

D-61

D-62

D-63

D-64

D-65

ANALOGIES

FIGURAL ANALOGIES—FOLLOW THE RULE

Read the rule above each box. Complete each pair in these analogies by drawing shapes that follow the rule.

D-66　Reduce size and color opposite.

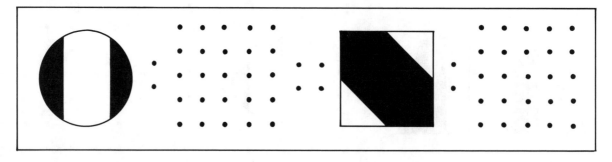

D-67　Increase size and rotate clockwise (⌒→) once.

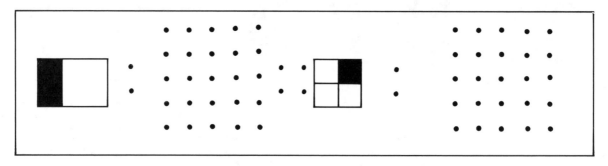

D-68　Reflect about the vertical and reduce size.

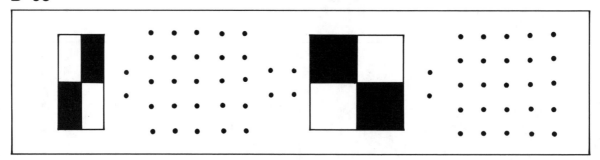

D-69　Increase size and reduce detail or number of parts.

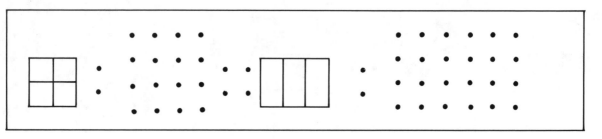

FIGURAL ANALOGIES—FOLLOW THE RULE

Read the rule above each box. Complete each pair in these analogies by drawing shapes that follow the rule.

D-70   Rotate one position to the right and color opposite.

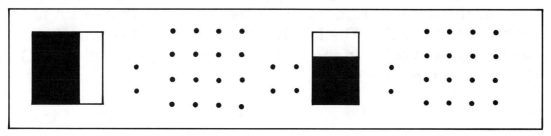

D-71   Reflect about the vertical and enlarge.

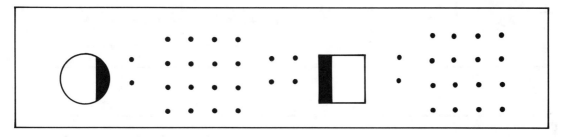

D-72   Reflect about the diagonal and decrease size.

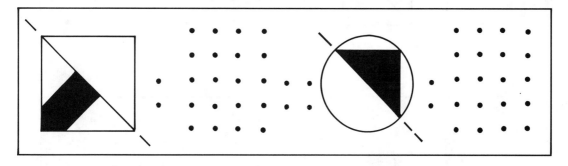

D-73   Reflect about the horizontal and color opposite.

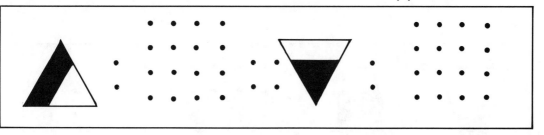

ANALOGIES

FIGURAL ANALOGIES—SUPPLY A PAIR

You have practiced doing figural analogies (A : B :: C : D) by drawing the last figure, D. Now you are asked to draw two missing figures, C and D.

Look at the first two figures (A and B) and notice how they are alike or different. Ask yourself, "What has been done to A to make it look like B?" The last two figures, C and D, should be related to each other in the same way that A is related to B. Draw C and D on the dot grid.

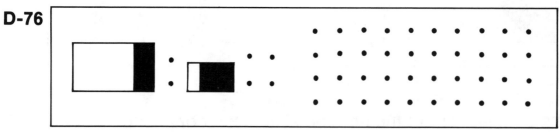

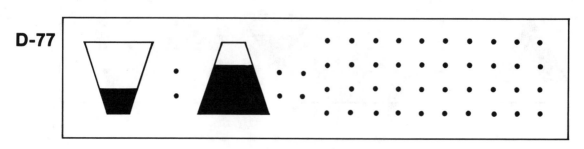

© 1985 MIDWEST PUBLICATIONS 93950

FIGURAL ANALOGIES—SUPPLY A PAIR

You have practiced doing figural analogies (A : B :: C : D) by drawing the last figure, D. Now you are asked to draw two missing figures, C and D.

Look at the first two figures (A and B) and notice how they are alike or different. Ask yourself, "What has been done to A to make it look like B?" The last two figures, C and D, should be related to each other in the same way that A is related to B. Draw C and D on the dot grid.

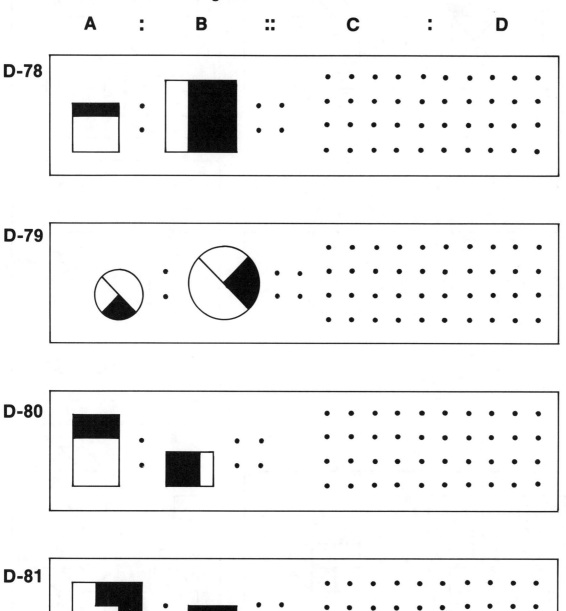

FIGURAL ANALOGIES—SELECT THE SOLID

Circle the figure that completes each figural analogy.

EXAMPLE:

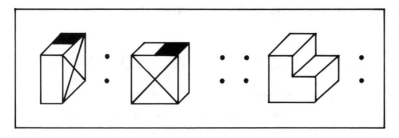
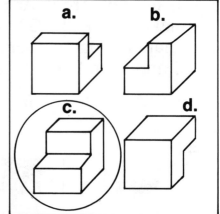

D-82

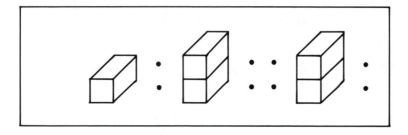
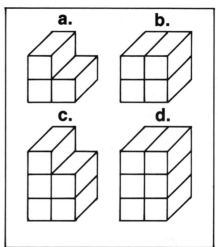

D-83

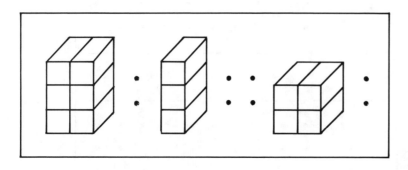
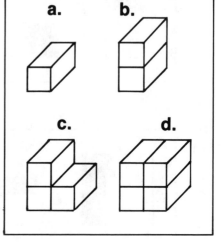

FIGURAL ANALOGIES—SELECT THE SOLID

Circle the figure that completes each figural analogy.

D-84

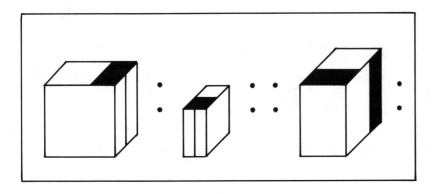

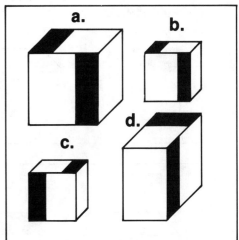

D-85

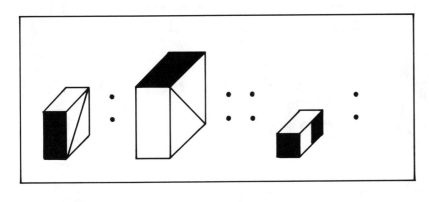

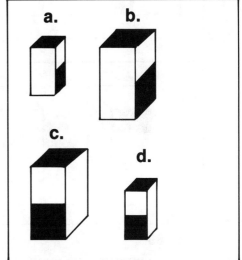

D-86

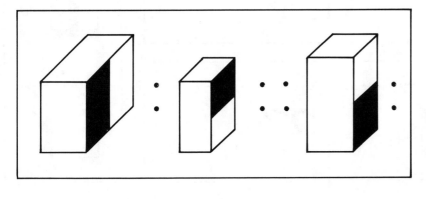

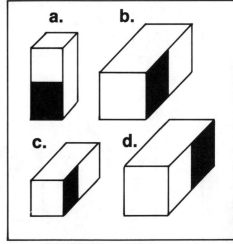

ANALOGIES

FIGURAL ANALOGIES—SELECT THE SOLID

Select the figure that completes the analogy. Write the letter for the correct figure on the line provided.

A   :   B   ::   C   :   D

EXAMPLE:

D-87

D-88

D-89

D-90

CHOICE BOX

a.

b.

c.

d.

e.

f.

FIGURAL ANALOGIES—SELECT THE SOLID

Select the figure that completes the analogy. Write the letter for the correct figure on the line provided.

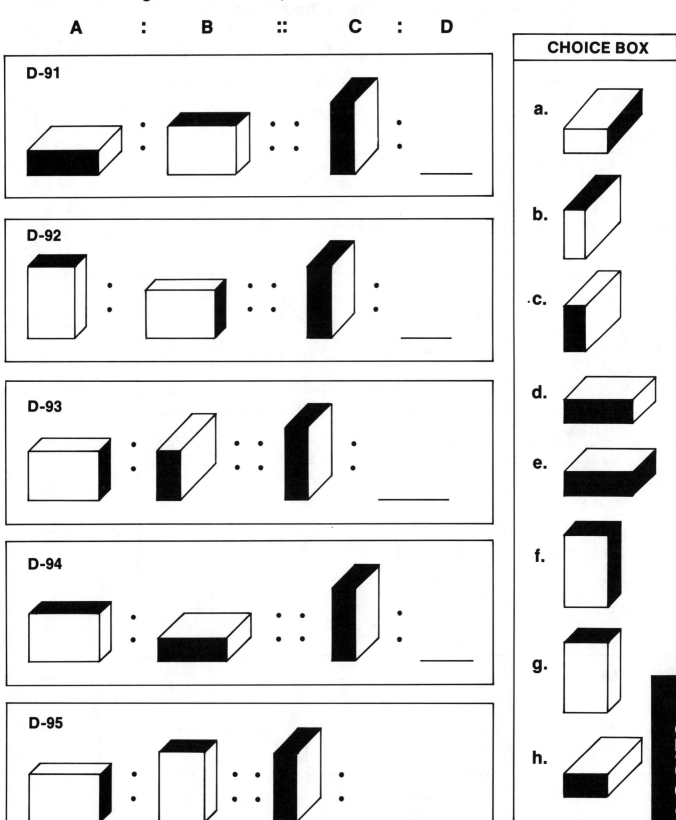

A   :   B   ::   C   :   D

CHOICE BOX

D-91

D-92

D-93

D-94

D-95

a.

b.

.c.

d.

e.

f.

g.

h.

ANALOGIES

FIGURAL ANALOGIES—SELECT THE SOLID

Select the figure that completes the analogy. Write the letter for
the correct figure on the line in the analogy.

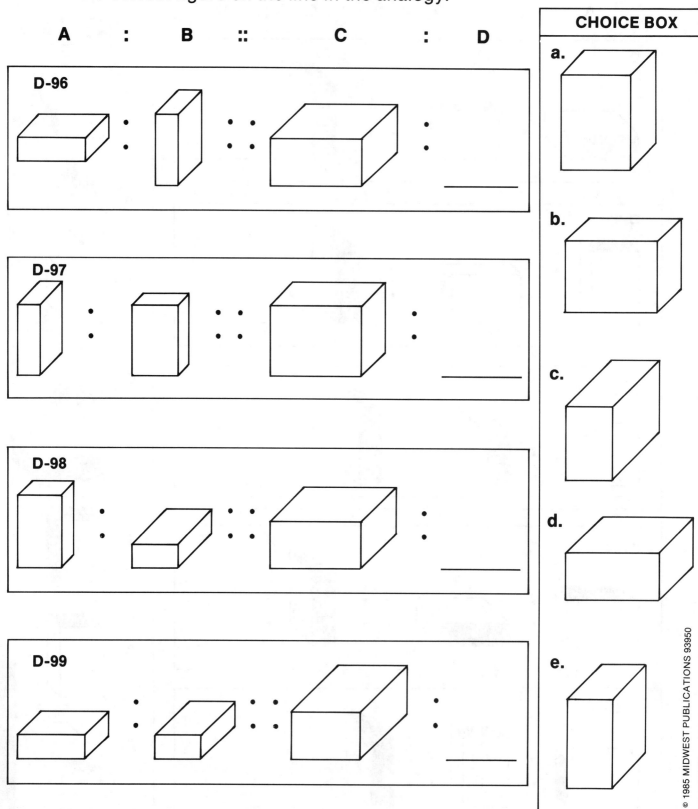

FIGURAL ANALOGIES—SELECT THE SOLID

Select the figure that completes the analogy. Write the letter for
the correct figure on the line in the analogy.

A　　:　　B　::　　C　　:　　D

CHOICE BOX

D-100

D-101

D-102

D-103

D-104

a.

b.

c.

d.

e.

f.

ANALOGIES

FIGURAL ANALOGIES—SELECT THE CUBE

Select the cube that completes the analogy. Write the letter for the correct cube on the line in the analogy.

In the following analogies involving rotating cubes, the cube is marked as shown.

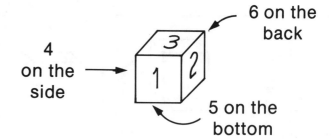

4 on the side

6 on the back

5 on the bottom

A : B :: C : D

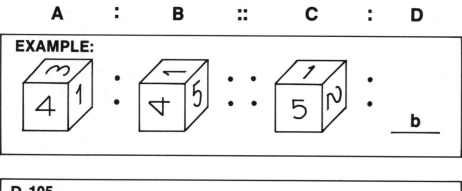

EXAMPLE:

b

D-105

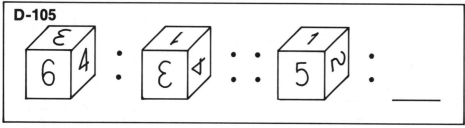

D-106

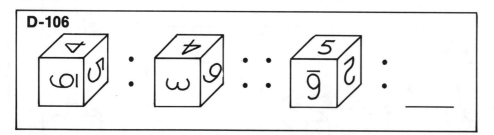

D-107

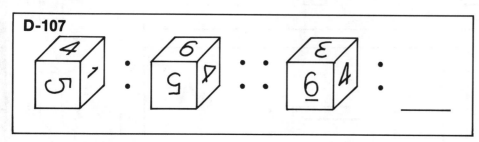

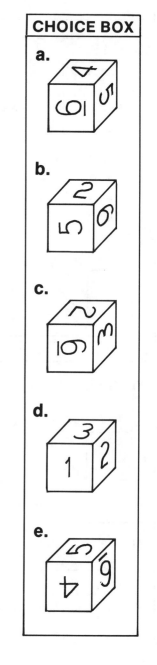

CHOICE BOX

a.

b.

c.

d.

e.